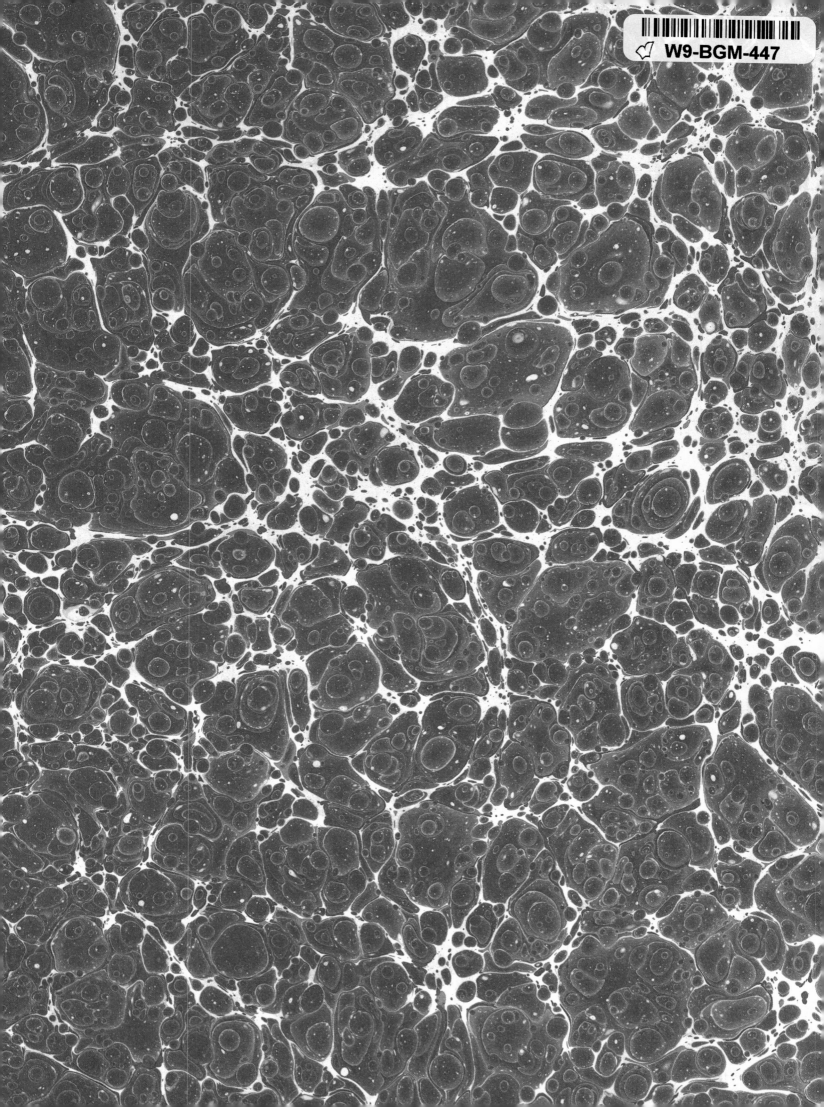

THE BOOK OF

AIR SHOWS

Philip Handleman

Foreword by Walter J. Boyne

Former Director of the National Air
and Space Museum, Smithsonian Institution

Schiffer Aviation History
Atglen, PA

Author's Note

Photographing air shows is for me both a joy and a challenge. When, for example, one of the military air demonstration team's approaches in a trademark formation, exuding extreme precision, my heart beats faster. Seconds later, at the moment all of the team's aircraft bank uniformly towards the audience in a majestic photo pass, I peer strenuously through a viewfinder and squeeze the shutter release button, hoping that aperture setting, shutter speed, composition, and focus will all gel to produce a picture that conveys a good measure of the drama I feel in person.

In this environment, obviously I do not control the action. I am a spectator, usually in the company of hundreds if not thousands of fellow enthusiasts, distinguished perhaps by the photographic equipment in my possession. I strive through my pictures, to capture air show performances as they occur before the eyes of those in attendance.

There is quite understandably a temptation to pose the beautiful show planes, be they restored warbirds or modern fighters, in photographs taken from the vantage point of a "photo ship" flying in close proximity. Such special photographic sessions are invariably pre-arranged with the performing pilots and almost always, for clear safety reasons, conducted away from the designated air show area or at a time when the air show is not in progress. The results of such photographic efforts are often stunning. I proudly display on my shelves many bound collections of these kinds of fine pictures.

But air show photography, in its truest form, is significantly different. In genuine air show photography the picture-taker is at the mercy of the performers. There is little if any opportunity for the photographer to stage the scene or to get the military team to repeat its photo pass of the day. The air show photographer is dealt a deck of cards and must make the most of it. Importantly, the pictures appearing in this volume, whether depicting static displays or flying acts, are authentic air show photographs.

I would be remiss if I did not acknowledge the contributions of my wife, Mary. A flyer by marriage, she has donned the seat-pack parachute in the front cockpit of the family Stearman and experienced the awe of flight from the invigorating vantage point of the fat-winged, wood and fabric, open biplane.

She has been my faithful sidekick at a multitude of air shows, sometimes having to settle for lodging accommodations never envisioned when, at our wedding, we mutually vowed "for better or worse . . ."

Always the curious one, she has tasted the fried artichokes at the Watsonville Fly-In. Under the blazing sun at the Reno Air Races, to keep us from dehydration, she has roamed until finding the soft drinks we like. She continues to marvel over the newly restored and freshly painted antique planes that have been meticulously brought back to life by dedicated craftsmen.

Mary has packed film, lugged cameras, and pointed to action that I would have otherwise missed. Along the way in this charmed adventure she has met some of the memorable personalities who populate the air show circuit. Her exposure to aviation in overwhelming doses now gives her the distinction of being able to identify many exotic airplanes, impressing her longtime friends who are expert in other disciplines.

Through it all, Mary has been an invaluable companion – my navigator in the air and on the ground. The air shows would not be the same without her.

Book Design by Robert Biondi

First Edition
Copyright © 1993 by Philip Handleman.
Library of Congress Catalog Number: 92-62187

Printed in the United States of America.
ISBN: 0-88740-471-5

We are interested in hearing from authors with book ideas on related topics.

Published by Schiffer Publishing Ltd.
77 Lower Valley Road
Atglen, PA 19310
Please write for a free catalog.
This book may be purchased from the publisher.
Please include $2.95 postage.
Try your bookstore first.

Foreword

The title THE BOOK OF AIR SHOWS is truly apt, for in photographs, words and spirit, Philip Handleman has captured the most thrilling – and most encouraging – elements of aviation in the world today. Ranging from ultra-lights to the huge transports, from warbirds to racers, Philip portrays aviation at its best – and at its most human.

A veteran of the air show circuit himself, Philip goes to the heart of the matter with both his camera and his captions, and he clearly understands that the beautifully finished aircraft and the dazzling aerobatic routines are merely symbols for the people who provide them, the same people who are nurturing flying at a time when it is beset by regulations and rising costs.

This book vividly portrays the remarkable egalitarian nature of the modern air show scene. At festivals – and that's the right term, for the mood is joyous – like the Experimental Aircraft Association's Oshkosh Fly-In, Sun 'n Fun or the Reno Air Races, it doesn't matter who you are or how much money you have; what matters are the skills you have brought to the sport, the care with which you've restored an antique, the help that you've rendered another, or just the interest you have in the sport. This spirit reaches across international and political boundaries as more and more participants are welcomed from all over the world; the utter enthusiasm with which participants from the former Soviet Union has been greeted is particularly symbolic.

The popularity of air shows cuts across the boundaries of age and gender as well, for they combine nostalgia and forward thinking in a way not found in other disciplines, and they offer everyone the opportunity to participate. The replication of a World War I fighter generates the same degree of interest as the debut of a new all-composite canard surfaced plane of the future.

Air shows have become the common denominator of aviation, a means by which the public can reach back to the glories of the flying past, while still looking ahead to future developments. In his superb THE BOOK OF AIR SHOWS, Philip Handleman offers an inspiring summary of the sport.

Walter J. Boyne

Dedication

*To the memory of
John D. "Lewk" Lewkowicz,
air show pilot and friend*

Contents

Introduction

The moment at which I became enamored of air shows is not exactly clear. Growing up, I was treated to thrilling stories of Cleveland's National Air Races in the 1930s. My mother lived within walking distance of the airport in those days, and being a curious and venturesome girl she and her neighborhood friend, reputedly unabashed tomboys both, scaled the perimeter fence when no one was looking and thereby gained access to the show grounds.

In her stories, my mother imparted to me that same sense of awe, innocent and genuine, that overcame her as an impressionable youngster when she witnessed sleek, state-of-the-art racers streak around pylons at record-breaking speeds. She told of seeing Lindbergh, Rickenbacker, and Doolittle. But her favorite, she was always quick to remind me, was the dashing, mustachioed Roscoe Turner. The prize-winning race pilot wore jodhpurs and a tailor-made tunic. His smile was contagious; wherever he strode he radiated vigor and charm. For publicity, he was photographed in the company of a "pet" lion.

When she went to work at that historic airport later in the decade, the airline pilots, by her description, were of a special breed – possessing some of that flair for adventure, that gutsy, romantic spirit embodied in the great Roscoe Turner. The flyers that my mother came to know at Hopkins Airport were all real stick and rudder men who had flown in the Great War, carried the mail or criss-crossed the country barnstorming. They had been navigating in the air from open cockpit days. To have made it this far they had to have been rugged individualists, imbued with strong self-confidence.

Although it sounds funny today, my mother disclosed in unreserved seriousness how she and her co-workers were absolutely stunned the first time their line landed a Douglas DC-3 at Hopkins. How could such a giant vehicle, all shiny metal, lift itself into the sky loaded with twenty-one passengers, baggage, fuel, and mail, they asked themselves incredulous.

As I approached adolescence, America, alarmed over the success of Sputnik, embarked on its noble experiment to propel humans beyond the atmosphere, into the exciting new frontier of space. The seven men selected to be our country's first explorers in this eerie and uncharted environment were all military pilots, the best of the best.

I have to the present admired the skill and courage of these first astronauts. They were my boyhood heroes. I became so overtly intrigued by the manned space program that my school's vice principal, a stern man not given to bending the rules, actually called me out of class into the privacy of his office to watch live television coverage of the Redstone and Atlas boosters blasting my idols into space.

I implored my parents to take me to an airport so that I could have the experience of sitting in a cockpit and feeling the sensation of flying. I will never forget that marvelous Sunday afternoon when they drove their twelve year-old son to the airstrip at Chagrin Falls, a quaint pasture with a few ramshackle hangars, mechanics roaming about in stained coveralls. Everywhere you looked were yellow, fabric-covered, and oil splattered Piper Cubs. This was paradise.

The pilot, a retired airline captain in uniform, gave me the remarkable opportunity once we were airborne to take the control stick of our docile Cub. For the next ten minutes I tried some turns, left and right. I think he let me climb and descend as well. With a tip of the captain's cap, I, the happiest little flyer in the world, was returned to my folks.

I must have been petulant for every time an air show came to town, I persuaded my parents to take me. How memorable was the tumultuous roar of the six Super Sabres of the Air Force Thunderbirds. Sweeping across the sky in impeccable formations, the team's pilots showed a graceful precision. While to them I was just another dot among the hundred thousand spectators, these men of the air, exceedingly accomplished in their profession, served to further inspire me.

As if addicted, I had to hang around airports, watching airplanes takeoff and land, helping to push an old taildragger out of the hangar, breathing the fuel vapors that wafted over the asphalt parking apron, listening to the oldtimers embellish stories of their flying past. Every airport has its special finds, and how wonderful it was when the airport's T-6 Texan, the famous World War II advanced trainer, would taxi out and give all of us bystanders an unexpected show. Tattered with age, the T-6 was nevertheless an airplane to behold. When it revved up at high RPM for the takeoff roll, it commanded your attention. The neighbors railed against the noise; I loved it.

It seemed that all rural airstrips then were destined to have a Stearman in residence. The big, open cockpit biplane with its radial engine was an instant conversation piece. Here was an airplane that captured the essence of what flying is all about. The pilot is exposed to the onrushing air, he can feel the chill and hear the wind. Travel is low and slow, the earth hardly moves, the aroma of the farmlands and sawmills drifts up and envelops the airplane. The pilot is one with the sky.

I spent hours gazing at these machines. Interestingly, I noticed that when a visitor caught sight of a Stearman, he would, whether or not he was an aviation aficionado, brighten up, a smile temporarily overtaking his demeanor. Yes, I could tell that these airplanes have a magic quality.

No wonder, then, that since World War II the Stearman has been the aircraft of choice for air show performers. It can be outfitted with a bigger, more powerful engine, a smoke system, and other modifications to make it sparkle before air show audiences. The Stearman, thusly upgraded, is capable of almost any aerobatic maneuver the performers can devise. Some titillate the crowds by carrying wingwalkers on their Stearmans, much as the gypsy pilots of the Golden Age of Flight did on their underpowered and flimsy Jennys.

This zestful world of air shows has for me come to epitomize humankind's love affair with flight. The best of aviation comes alive at air shows. The most beautiful airplanes are exhibited and the greatest flying practitioners display their expert skills. Fly-ins, an outgrowth of air shows, bring together people who share a common interest. Not surprisingly, life long friendships have evolved from these unpretentious gatherings. Now, in the pages that follow, let us retrace that pleasurable and inspiring path as we tour the air show/fly-in circuit.

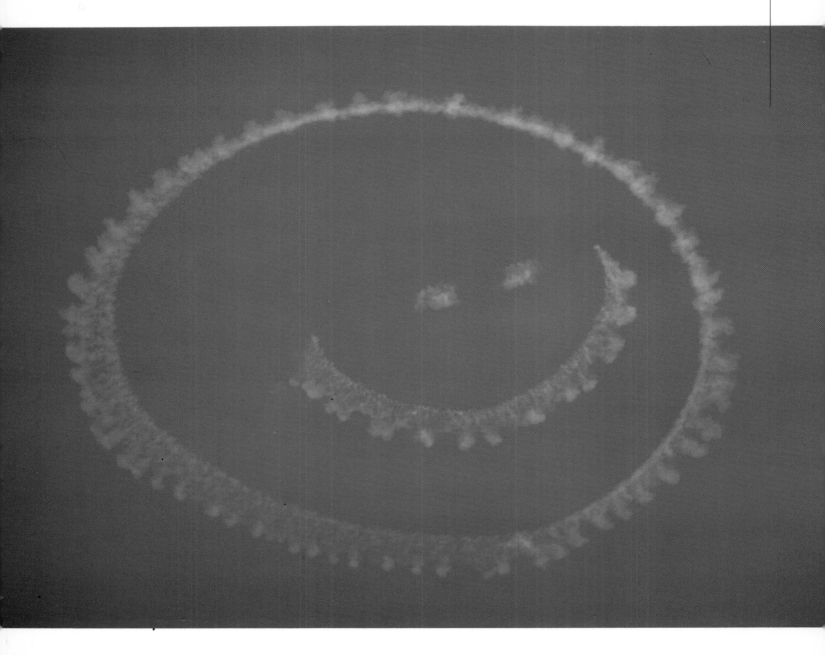

Skywriting, masterfully executed in the serene skies high above Lakeland, Florida, provides a fitting dimension to the opening ceremonies of the popular Sun 'n Fun Fly-In. For years, Steve Oliver and his wife Suzanne Asbury-Oliver have perpetuated the dying art of skywriting. Using an old Travel Air biplane, they fly through the sky emitting plumes of white smoke in a seemingly effortless ballet that produces letters and symbols as neat as anyone with an award in penmanship. Their jovial creature, as depicted in this picture, grins approvingly on the fly-in festivities about to begin. (Sun 'n Fun, 1987)

Chapter I

Ragwing Regalia

Old-time flying, the way barnstormers took to the air, with the wind whistling across the bracing wires and a silk scarf flapping in the slipstream, lives on today because of the efforts of a hardy troop of aviation enthusiasts. Working unheralded in a barn on the Kansas prairie or at an airstrip carved out of a Nebraska cornfield or behind the garage at the family farm in Idaho, antiquers, wherever they may be, labor intensely to keep alive a vestige of aviation's exciting and dramatic past. Applying the production techniques of generations ago, forming tubular metal, sanding wood, and stitching fabric, they bring back to airworthy condition relics thought abandoned for good. In some of these restoration projects the patience of Job is required. The reward comes on the day the object of all the commotion – the innumerable man-hours of work, the weeks spent tracking down a rare part, the neighbor running over to lend a tool – is rolled out and returned, after a lengthy absence, to the inviting sky. The craftsmanship and finishes in the current spate of ragwing beauties are unequaled, rivaling the purity of the factory-new versions from sixty and seventy years earlier. Air shows and fly-ins brim with a nostalgic flavorfulness thanks to the dedication of the antiquer community. The radial-engined, open cockpit biplanes characteristic of wood and fabric days, reborn in stunning paint schemes, are a sight uplifting to the spirit.

Typically, the Memorial Day holiday is punctuated with air shows and fly-ins across the country. For families out on a weekend drive, the hand-painted roadside sign advertising an aviation happening at the local airport can be a powerful lure. Since 1964 the Northern California Antique Airplane Association has put on a splendid event at the quaint and agreeable Watsonville Municipal Airport. (Watsonville, 1989)

The Watsonville Fly-In, though still largely a regional gathering, has emerged as a prestigious annual showcase for many dozens of unbelievably immaculate wood and fabric restorations. Radial engines are notorious for spitting oil which then splatters on the belly of a biplane's linen covered fuselage. Yet, at Watsonville, as if by some unspoken law, the antiquers come with aircraft that appear too clean to have been flown. For every hour in the air, the owners toil two hours or more wiping the glorious plane down with mineral spirits and all variety of cleanser. As spectators amble past, awed by the sparkling beauties arrayed on the impromptu parking ramps, the arm-weary owners may break from their tedious chores to acknowledge glowing praise. Watsonville's colorful mix of antiques can be seen here. (Watsonville, 1991)

Above: Introduced as a primary trainer for the military in World War II, the Boeing Stearman Model 75 came to embody the spirit of flight. By war's end it had taught more cadets how to fly than any other airplane. Unlike its wartime brethren, the Stearman was resurrected in the civilian world as an agricultural applicator. When new environmental regulations eliminated the open cockpit relics from the sprayer fleet, the Stearman discovered yet another purpose in life. Currently satisfying perhaps its highest calling, the Stearman, with air show modifications like constant-speed propeller, upper wing ailerons, and smoke system, injects the feel of old-time barnstorming. This substantially beefed up Stearman, being tended to by a diligent field maintenance crew, is the mount of well-known West Coast performer, Eddie Andreini. (Watsonville, 1989)

OVERLEAF:
The Stearman was designed to impart the fundamentals of flying including rudimentary aerobatics. Eddie Andreini's Stearman, seen here streaking straight up over the Watsonville Municipal Airport, is able to sustain vertical flight longer than a stock Stearman because of its many performance modifications.

Top left: At the top of the vertical climb, as air speed bleeds off and the stall approaches, Eddie jams the left rudder pedal and slides the control stick to starboard, implementing a crisp hammerhead turn. *Top right*: All one and a half tons of the burly Stearman convulse violently as the ship is thrusted through the rigors of a lomchevak, an East European maneuver roughly translated as "headache." The wild twists and turns have backed the biplane into the cloud created by its own smoke system. At this point, the pilot is helpless and has to wait until his aircraft loses inertia. Only when the Stearman falls out of the maneuver is Eddie able to regain control. *Bottom left*: Almost as if suspended in the sky, this beefed up World War II trainer is captured at the moment when the sun's rays are blocked by the lower wing and tail surfaces, casting a curious shadow against the smoke that trails backwards. *Bottom right*: No matter how good the pilot, Newton's laws still apply. After climbing straight up, Eddie's big biplane reverses its course, plummeting back to earth tail first, but soon flopping over nose first. Here Eddie exits a tailslide. With a nonstop routine where the aircraft never seems to rest, Eddie keeps the eyes of his audience glued to the sky. His act is a regular highlight at the Watsonville Fly-In. (All photos, Watsonville, 1989)

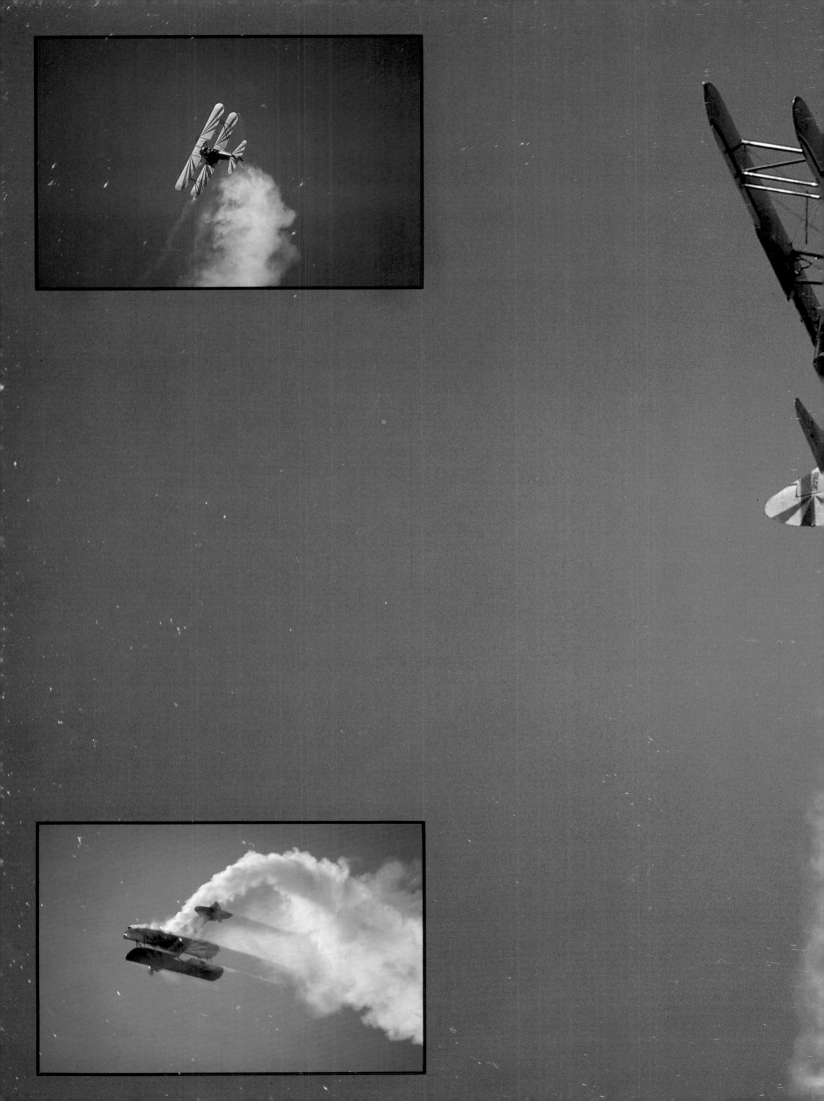

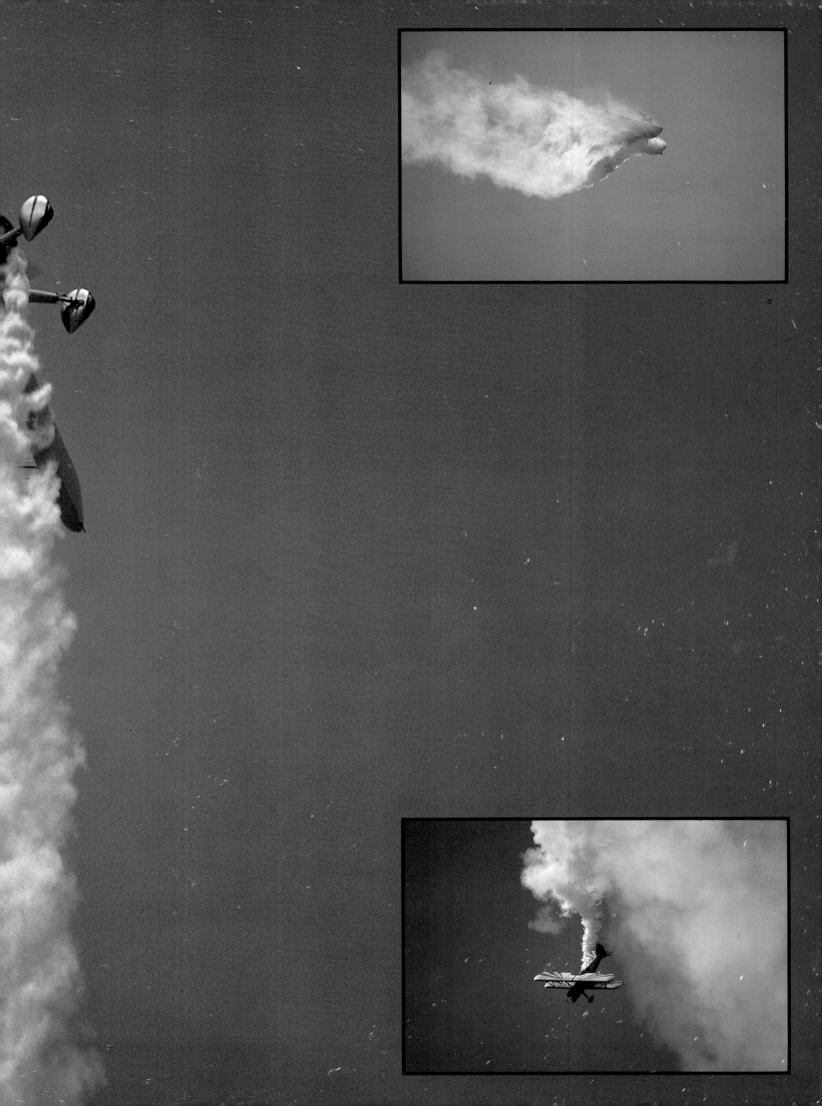

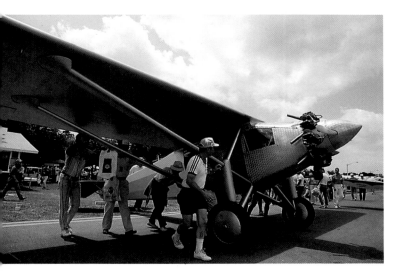

Left: The Experimental Aircraft Association is, among other objectives, dedicated to preserving aviation's heritage. It does so, in part, by devoting countless man-hours to restoring or replicating historic planes. Seen here being gently pushed by a cadre of eager volunteers is the EAA's second flying replica of Charles Lindbergh's famed SPIRIT OF SAINT LOUIS. By being able to get up close to a superbly re-created Ryan NYP, people can better appreciate the dedication, stamina, and courage of the "Lone Eagle" when he soloed across the Atlantic in May 1927. (Sun 'n Fun, 1992)

Below: The showplane area at Sun 'n Fun is replete with rare gems. This neat little biplane is an Arrow Sport, an early sportsman's aircraft, featuring spoked wheels and ever so romantic side-by-side seating for two. (Sun 'n Fun, 1992)

OPPOSITE:

Above: Conjuring up images of Manfred von Richthofen, the "Red Baron", is this sparkling replica of the World War I Fokker Dr I Triplane. Hardly a wise camouflage paint scheme, the vibrant red covering projected the top ace's persona. The plane itself offered a skilled pilot like von Richthofen an extremely maneuverable weapons platform. Today, on the air show circuit no one need dodge this Fokker triple decker. It is a form of history that has come to life. (Watsonville, 1989)

Below: Among Germany's more effective fighters during World War I was the streamlined Albatros. This stunning replica is part of a growing collection based at Guntersville, Alabama. On one of its first outings, this fragile replica is taxiied, ever so carefully and with linemen at the wingtips, to the Sun 'n Fun flight line at Lakeland, Florida. (Sun 'n Fun, 1992)

When not mesmerizing air show crowds with his performances in the Pepsi Sky Dancer (a souped up de Havilland Chipmunk), air show veteran Steve Oliver introduces throngs of patrons to their first open cockpit ride in a spectacularly restored New Standard. With matching automobile by the ticket table, Steve's wife, Suzanne Asbury-Oliver, has no problem selling out the available space in the front cockpit when the weather is accommodating at Sun 'n Fun. The Olivers' plane is ideal for giving rides since the passenger cockpit can hold up to three people, making each circuit around the pattern a more lucrative exercise. The announcement emblazoned on the bottom of the lower wings also serves to drum up business. (Sun 'n Fun, 1991)

The intriguing part of journeying to air shows and fly-ins is the unexpected find that surfaces amid the rows of familiar showplanes. New to the circuit is the amazing replica of the Gee Bee R-2 racer. This replica, built by Delmar Benjamin and Steve Wolf, is almost an exact re-creation of the plane produced in 1932 by the Granville Brothers. The Gee Bees were noted for their difficult and unforgiving handling characteristics, but at a growing number of air shows Delmar has deftly controlled the mighty little demon performing rolls, knife edge flight, and even inverted ribbon cuts. (Sun 'n Fun, 1992)

During the annual week-long EAA Convention in Oshkosh which ordinarily attracts upwards of 800,000 visitors, a tiny airport within an airport rests all but obscured behind the EAA's sprawling Air Adventure Museum. Tucked away in a corner of Oshkosh's Wittman Regional Airport is the EAA's re-creation of a country airport from a bygone era. Known as Pioneer Airport, the mini-field has its own grass airstrip, which is especially suitable for the restored wood and fabric airplanes hangared there as part of the EAA's impressive collection. Although this little field is not operated during the Convention, on weekends from spring through fall the charming antiques in the collection are brought out and flown. (Oshkosh, 1989)

The biplane justifiably evokes a sense of nostalgia. Indeed, the first successful powered aircraft, the Wright Flyer, was a biplane. The choice of truss construction for the wings insured the bi-plane's sturdiness. Staggering the wings could also delay the onset of aerodynamic stall. Eventually the biplane gave way to the predominance of the monoplane, but not before innovations like aileron connector struts added for faster roll response and cockpit canopies mounted to shield the pilot from the harsh elements. (Oshkosh, 1989)

An honored place for those dedicated souls who labor for innumerable hours bringing back to life in exquisite grandeur the exhumed hulks and forgotten "basket cases" of aviation's past is the Circle of Past Grand Champions shown here at Sun 'n Fun. The experienced, hands-on EAA judges pick Grand Champions in several categories each year. On return in subsequent years, the winners are accorded this special parking area. Roped off behind the sign is a magnificent Beech Staggerwing. (Sun 'n Fun, 1991)

Conceived in Wichita in the 1930s, the Beech Staggerwing with its teardrop shape, "I" struts, negative wing stagger, retractable landing gear, and spacious cabin offered well-to-do customers a taste of the future. Streamlined and powerful, the Staggerwing could overtake most military planes of its day. A whole new standard was set for personal and business flying with the introduction of this advanced design. Today the Staggerwing is a collector's item, valued at many times the Beech factory's original list, to be pampered by the owner and admired by the spectator. (Watsonville, 1989)

Right: The Stearman is found in legend as much as any airplane ever built. Because it was the U.S. military's leading primary trainer of World War II, the pilots from that era fondly recall the Stearman. It was an airplane that kept you on your toes, particularly when landing as it has closely coupled main gear, a high center of gravity, and there is no forward visibility over the round engine out front. If you were not careful, the big biplane would veer off the edge of the runway in a goundloop. Because of its rugged construction, your pride was likely to suffer more than any part of your anatomy in such a landing accident. Nevertheless, the Stearman was an honest airplane. If you treated it with respect, it would return the favor. This Stearman, painted in unconventional though striking colors, is shown at the first annual National Biplane Association Fly-In in Bartlesville, Oklahoma in 1987. (Bartlesville, 1987)

With about 10,000 Stearmans built and their widespread employment in the agricultural industry, it is not surprising that they are today's most prevalent open cockpit biplane. This example is an air show conversion and was flown by the great Bill Barber. In more recent years it has been skillfully flown on the circuit by Bob Barden of Ann Arbor, Michigan. (Oshkosh, 1989)

Right: Every year near Labor Day, scores of Stearmans from around the country, sometimes more than one hundred, convene in the small west central Illinois town of Galesburg. There, the Stearman owners revel in not merely the brotherhood of those who fly but in their common bond of knowing the exhileration of open cockpit flight. Activities include flying contests, breakfasts, and a dawn patrol, but there is also time to wander between the rows of shining restorations, looking out over the unspoiled corn fields that encompass the quaint airport, just savoring the tranquility and wholesomeness as if detached from the larger world. A Stearman in its glory – on grass in calm wind with a blue sky overhead. (Galesburg, 1987)

Left: While the Army and Navy utilized the Stearman as a primary trainer during World War II, they adopted different paint schemes. The early Army Stearmans were painted with a blue fuselage and yellow wings, whereas the Navy Stearmans were painted all yellow. The Army referred to the Stearman as the Kaydet, and the Navy nicknamed it, for obvious reasons, the Yellow Peril. (Watsonville, 1991)

Husband and wife wingwalking team Earl and Paula Cherry have delighted air show audiences around the country with their aerial antics. Earl is flying inverted so much of the time that his name is emblazoned upside down on the fuselage of his highly modified Stearman. Paula is supported by a vertical brace firmly anchored to the upper wing's center section. Like the barnstormers from the Golden Age of Flight who exposed themselves to the unrelenting onrushing wind, Paula is subjected to the irrepressibly strong slipstream. Much practice and exercise allow her to pose in a seemingly effortless manner. A small number of other wingwalking teams keeps alive the barnstorming spirit. (Flint, 1987)

OPPOSITE:

Above: In the primary trainer parking section at Geneseo is this radiant de Havilland Tiger Moth. This plane was to the British what the Stearman was to the American military training effort. Though diminutive in comparison with its American cousin, the Tiger Moth effectively imparted the basics of flying including the garden variety of aerobatics to Royal Air Force trainees. Thousands of pilots from World War II have a soft spot in their hearts for the little plane that initiated them into the world of stick and rudder skills. (Geneseo, 1990)

Below: Before the formal air show at Watsonville, a constant procession of antiques fills the sky. In the course of the morning cavalcade it is likely that airplanes of varying milieu will share the same patch of sky. Here, two beautiful restorations, a Tiger Moth and a cabin Waco, formate during a pass. (Watsonville, 1991)

The gullwing of the Stinson Reliant is apparent in this view. Dozens of glorious restorations like the one shown here occupy the showplane parking area at Watsonville. Each year the judges are faced with the difficult task of selecting the best restoration. Their choice receives the Fly-In's Grand Champion Award. Custom then dictates that the winning plane's image be reproduced on the following year's T-shirts, printed programs, coffee mugs, and lapel pins. These forms of recognition are an incentive to restorers seeking to enter their handiwork in the Watsonville competition. (Watsonville, 1989)

PREVIOUS:
This is the scene at the annual warbirds show at the Geneseo Airport in upstate New York as the primary trainers line up to depart on the 5,000-foot long grass runway. Aircraft matched by type fly orbits in loose formation around the field as part of the air show. The informal flavor of this event is unusual for a warbird show. Behind the biplanes is a Texan advanced trainer. (Geneseo, 1990)

If it were not for the dedicated restoration efforts of the antiquers combined with the staging of many fly-ins and air shows, vital parts of aviation history would perhaps not be forgotten but would certainly become stale. This clever piece of airplane trim, appropriately glistening in the sun, is a reminder of the important aeronautical contributions of Giuseppe Bellanca, a talented aircraft designer during the halcyon years of the Golden Age of Flight. (Sun 'n Fun, 1989)

The ubiquitous Piper Cub, though small in physical size was unquestionably a giant in its impact on aviation. The light, 65 hp J-3 that rolled out of William T. Piper's Lock Haven, Pennsylvania plant offered the common man the means to fly. It was a simple (to borrow from today's jargon, "user friendly") airplane to fly and economical to operate. The Cub made the weekend pilot a reality, and all across the country from rural grass strips to major terminals the little, all yellow Pipers with their distinctive tail-mounted emblem populated the aviation landscape. (Sun 'n Fun, 1989)

Showing the extent to which antiquers may go in restoring their beloved airplanes is this view of the cockpit of a rare Luscombe Sedan. The instrument panel is almost entirely authentic and without even a smudge on the gauges and dials. The interior has been reupholstered in a coordinated two-tone fabric matching the plane's paint finish. Such attention to detail warms the hearts of aviation enthusiasts who, with the owner's permission, may step over the rope and gaze into a cabin that resembles a factory new product. (Watsonville, 1989)

There are only two of the stainless steel amphibious Fleetwings Seabirds flying. This one, based along Florida's east coast, regularly graces the Sun 'n Fun Fly-In with its presence. In the quiet morning hours of spring, as the early sun slowly burns off the lingering fog, pilots and airplane buffs rub their eyes, awaken, and emerge from the camp-grounds to capture the sight of a seldom seen airplane silhouetted against the horizon. That is what fly-ins and air shows are about. (Sun 'n Fun, 1989)

The Lockheed P-38 Lightning is a design marvel. Conceived in the 1930s by Lockheed's design genius Clarence "Kelly" Johnson, the P-38 incorporated a twin-boom configuration with its two liquid-cooled engines turning contra-rotating propellers. This eliminated the ordinary tendency of an aircraft's nose to yaw left because of torque effect. Accordingly, the P-38 was an unusually stable gun platform with its heavy firepower concentrated in its nose, directly in line with the pilot. The aircraft had a bubble-type canopy from the outset of its production run, giving the pilot 360 degree visibility. The plane also sported tricycle landing gear, a rarity in those days. Because the P-38 was so sleek and so powerfully propelled, it was among the earliest of airplanes to encounter the phenomenon of compressibility – hitting shock waves near the speed of sound. Here well-known racing pilot Lefty Gardner is seen putting his nearly all white P-38, called WHITE LIT'NIN, through its paces. (Reno, 1987)

Chapter II

Warbird Wonders

The airplane, with all its intrinsic beauty, has frequently in its short ninety years of existence undergone the transformation to an instrument of war. Not surprisingly, when aircraft designers have confronted the urgency imposed by the starkness of human conflict on a grand scale, they have responded with alacrity. Indeed, as if proving the veracity of the old adage that necessity is the mother of invention, the greatest and most rapid advances in aeronautical technology have occurred during times of war. Coupled with unprecedented progress in structures and engines, World War II saw the application of Henry Ford's production line manufacturing savvy to the construction of airplanes. Defense plants geared up and at their peak were churning out airplanes by the tens of thousands. At war's end, many of the combat aircraft that survived the multitudinous hazards of battle fell victim to the accountant's pen and were consigned to desert boneyards for eventual scrapping. Where once there may have been 5,000 or 10,000 or 15,000 of a particular type of aircraft that in squadron after squadron would fill the sky, there is now only a tiny remnant. Fortunately, samplings of the heavy iron from World War II are kept flying by diehard volunteers connected with organizations like the Confederate Air Force, the National Warplane Museum, the Valiant Air Command, the Yankee Air Force, the Canadian Warplane Heritage, and the Experimental Aircraft Association's Warbirds of America.

The annual Valiant Air Command warbird air show in early April signals the start of the air show season. The VAC is a non-profit organization committed to preserving World War II vintage combat planes. Its extravagant air show with ground-ignited pyrotechnics boasts the largest contingent of warbirds of any show in the Southeast. This is the VAC's emblem, an eagle clutching lightning bolts and superimposed against a "V" with the organization's title spelled out below. Many of the warbirds in attendance sport this symbol of the VAC. (Tico, 1987)

Trainers

Up until recent years, the site of the VAC warbird air show was known as the Titusville-County Airport. It was usually abbreviated as "Tico" Airport. But the local politicos felt this name did not do the facility justice as it was the closest civil airport to the Kennedy Space Center, a major tourist attraction in its own right. To reflect the airport's proximity to the world famous NASA launch facility, the name was officially changed to Space Center Executive Airport. Nevertheless, air show regulars are stuck in the habit of calling the airport and its annual air show merely Tico. A volunteer is shown here directing visitors to the ticket booth for flight line passes. (Tico, 1989)

During World War II, when U.S. military cadets successfully completed primary and basic flight training, they moved up to the final phase before obtaining their wings. In this stage of their training they encountered the North American T-6 Texan. Powered by a brutish 600 hp Pratt & Whitney engine that whipped around the comparatively short propeller blades at near supersonic speed causing a distinctive raspiness that could be heard far and wide, this advanced trainer humbled many a cocky student. Unlike the docile planes in the primary phase, the T-6 was fast and it forced the cadets to contend with such complex systems as a constant speed propeller, wing flaps, retractable landing gear, etc. If they could handle this demanding machine, the aspiring pilots got their wings. (Tico, 1989)

On today's air show scene T-6s are a common sight. They have been restored in all imaginable colors, but some owners have chosen to polish the bare metal leaving the skin of the fine-lined, angular aircraft as shown here. On a bright day, you can see the plane's fuselage reflected in the wing. The enormous amount of waxing and buffing it takes to make this possible is a tribute to the fastidious owner. (Sun 'n Fun, 1989)

A Texan rolls gracefully through the afternoon sky, exhibiting its acknowledged aerobatic prowess. North American's advanced trainer found favor with both the Army and Navy. In Navy service, the aircraft was designated the SNJ. The trainer shown here is emblazoned with the alternating black and white D-Day invasion stripes outboard from the wing roots, a liberty taken by the owner. (Tico, 1989)

The trusty de Havilland Chipmunk gave British trainees the underlying skills they would need to fly the combat aircraft in the RAF's inventory. Interestingly, the Chipmunk's performance characteristics are such that the parkers at Sun 'n Fun typically direct attending Chipmunks like this one to the antique/classic area. The effervescent yellow training color is a marked contrast to the more prosaic schemes of the surrounding planes. (Sun 'n Fun, 1992)

A T-28 Trojan banks steeply, its powerful engine reverberating distinctively. The familiar churning drone of Trojans hauling through the sky is music to the ears of air show attendees. The good visibility provided by the bubble canopy along with exemplary maneuverability made the T-28 a candidate for counter-insurgency ground attack operations during the Vietnam War. A modified version of the aircraft was produced for this mission and deployed in combat. It was effective in the hunter-killer mission, unleashing its significant weapons payload on targets marked by forward air controllers. (Chino, 1989)

Although the Beech T-34 is not as big or as loud as the T-28 Trojan, it has enjoyed remarkable longevity. The Mentor, as the T-34 is known, dates to the 1950s as a primary trainer for both the Air Force and Navy. While the former eventually opted to begin training its flight students on jets, the latter stuck with the Mentor, albeit the turboprop C model. Shown here are two of the earlier piston-powered T-34s that fly as part of a larger Mentor formation team. The surplus Mentors in civilian hands that fly on the air show circuit have steadily escalated in price as they are considered paragons of practicality. They are warbirds and can be flown aerobatically, yet they possess the fine cross-country flying qualities and economy of operation associated with Beech's ultimate businessman's piston single, the Bonanza. (Tico, 1987)

OPPOSITE:

Above: Cessna's innocent-looking, almost cartoonish, Bobcat was a twin-engine trainer. Before taking the yoke of the heavies, the principles of multi-engine operation were learned in this plane, as well as in competing Beech and Curtiss models. Because of the Cessna's extensive use of wood in construction, the aircraft was sometimes called the Bamboo Bomber. (Watsonville, 1989)

Below: The last of the American military's radial engined trainers, the North American T-28 sits high off the ground and thereby gives some pilots the sensation of riding on an imposing charger as knights of old. (Tico, 1989)

Fighters

Below: This Mustang, its polished skin aglitter, bakes in the Nevada desert awaiting another speed trial at the Reno Air Races. Whereas the Mustangs of old, the nearly 16,000 built during World War II, were commonly dirtied in mud or dust while operating from grass strips in England or hastily prepared forward airfields on the Continent, the flying examples of today are generally as pristine and spotless as the day they rolled out of the factory. (Reno, 1989)

Right: Supermarine's brilliant young designer, Reginald J. Mitchell, was obsessed with achieving higher speed and concentrated on developing record-breaking aircraft for the Schneider Trophy seaplane races of the 1930s. His successful entries in those competitions led to his splendid Spitfire. Here the Spitfire wing's unique elliptical shape can clearly be seen as the airplane's underside planform view is exposed in a dramatic flyover. (Harlingen, 1989)

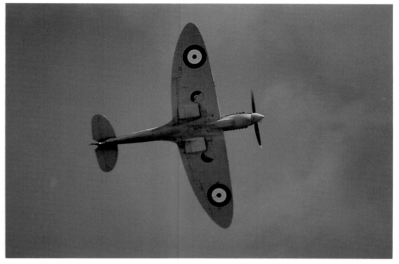

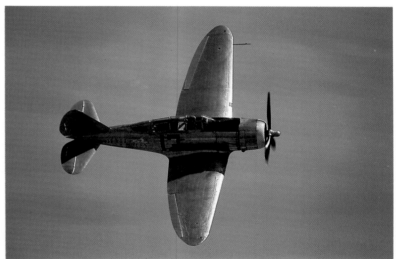

The Seversky was a pre-World War II fighter design that was on the cutting edge of 1930s aeronautical technology. Designed by the Russian emigre Alexander Seversky, the plane attained fame as a worthy competitor in air races. The aircraft served as the basis for the subsequent Republic P-47 Thunderbolt, the highly regarded, versatile World War II fighter. (Chino, 1989)

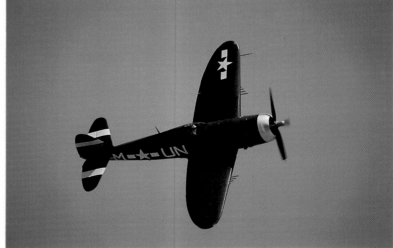

Perhaps more than any other Allied fighter of World War II, the P-47, shown here in knife-edge flight and closely resembling the streamlined shape of the Seversky, developed a reputation for being able to absorb the punishment of enemy firepower. Stories are legion of how the Jug, as the Thunderbolt was widely known, returned to base with chunks of engine cylinders or swaths of wing sections missing. (Chino, 1989)

The imposing spinner and propeller blades of the legendary North American P-51 Mustang are captured in this mid-day closeup. The Mustang was first supplied to the British. Disappointed with its performance, the Royal Air Force outfitted the early model with a Rolls Royce Merlin engine. The change in powerplant made a world of difference, and from that point the Mustang was destined to become a fighter pilot's dream. (Sun 'n Fun 1989)

PREVIOUS:

This is an unlikely formation – from the left, a British Spitfire, a Japanese Zero, a German (Spanish built) Messerschmitt, and an American Mustang. The organizers of the old Chino, Califormia warbird air shows would pull out the stops and would flood the skies with all variety of World War II combat planes during the massive weekend event. Here a leading fighter from each of the major combat theaters of World War II were brought together in an unforgettable formation. (Chino, 1989)

Inset: A closer view of the Spitfire and the Zero highlights the design similarities and contrasts in these two exceptional fighters. The Spitfire has a liquid-cooled engine versus the Zero's radial engine. The Spitfire's armament at first consisted of eight machine guns. Later, two 20 mm cannon and four .303-in machine guns became typical. The Zero had a combination of four cannon and machine guns. Both aircraft were highly maneuverable and responsive to pilot control inputs. (Chino, 1989)

The workhorse of the Luftwaffe's fighter forces was the Messerschmitt Bf 109. The example shown here is a Bf 109G supplied to the Spanish Air Force during World War II and redesignated the HA 1112. The Spanish versions of this aircraft were at first fitted with the 1,300 hp V12 Hispano-Suiza 12-Z-89 engine since the standard Daimler-Benz DB 605 engine was unavailable. In the 1950s Spanish versions were, ironically, equipped with a modified Rolls Royce Merlin engine. The Bf 109, light and maneuverable, was a feared adversary. However, as the war progressed the performance characteristics of the Bf 109 paled in comparison to newer designs. The aircraft's closely coupled landing gear and lack of forward visibility on landing make it a handful to control on the ground. This one which belongs to well-known aircraft broker Denny Sherman of West Palm Beach, Florida, is seen here being refueled after some low level air show passes. As one of the few flying Bf 109s in the world today, this example has not surprisingly appeared in several motion pictures about World War II aerial combat. (Tico, 1992)

Among the seven P-47s still flying is this superbly restored example, painstakingly rebuilt by owner Charles Osborn of Louisville, Kentucky to resemble the Thunderbolt flown by Howard M. Park of the 513th Squadron of the Ninth Air Force's 406th Fighter Group. Park rumbled through Europe in his plane, supporting General Patton's advancing columns. While his primary mission was to destroy enemy ground targets, he shot down two Messerschmitts. In the course of his exploits, Park's P-47 was badly shot up and he was wounded twice. He received many decorations for his courage and valor. The exquisite detail of this restoration, emphasizing authenticity, serves to attract air show spectators like a magnet and at the same time pays tribute to an American wartime flying hero. Quite properly, this former Venezuelan Air Force P-47 D-40, as lovingly restored by Charles Osborn, has won restoration awards at the two biggest fly-ins – Sun 'n Fun and Oshkosh. (Tico, 1992)

PREVIOUS:
Arguably the best all around Allied fighter of World War II, the North American P-51 Mustang is still frequently seen on the air show circuit as there are several dozen that actively participate in flying performances and at fly-ins. It has become common to decorate the surviving examples in the paint schemes of World War II squadrons and even in the colors of particular pilots. As can be seen here, this P-51 has been emblazoned with the alternating black and white D-Day invasion stripes. This was a simple means to alert Allied forces as to which planes were friendlies. (Mt. Comfort, 1987)

Left inset: Skimming the treetops is an understatement for this restored P-51, BALD EAGLE. A more apt description would be shaving the corn stalks as this Mustang roars over the nicely manicured 5,000-foot long grass runway of the Geneseo, New York, Airport. Home to the National Warplane Museum, the Geneseo facility each year hosts a "Wings of Eagles" air show that features a wide array of World War II era warbirds. Mustangs in the Korean War, by then designated F-51s, flew low level attacks carrying out strafing missions on enemy ground targets. The adaptability of Mustangs from interceptor to fighter escort to close air support is a tribute to their design. (Geneseo, 1990) *Right inset:* The Mustang, oddly enough, was conceived in response to British specifications before the U.S. was even drawn into World War II. In a dazzling display of American technological ingenuity, the Mustang went from drawing board concept to completed airframe in 117 days. Performance with the original Allison engine was improved with the installation of the superior Merlin engine. The design team headed by North American's Edgar Schmued developed in record time a highly advanced fighter that sported among other innovations a semi-laminar flow wing. The better cruise efficiency afforded by this airfoil design and the use of expendable fuel tanks enabled the Mustang to escort Eighth Air Force bombers on their long-range missions, reversing the devastating loss rates attributable to sharp-shooting enemy fighters. (Harlingen, 1989)

Many a World War II Navy and Marine Corps pilot who served in the Pacific will swear that the greatest piston-powered fighter plane ever built was the Vought F4U Corsair. Fitted with the giant 2,000 hp Pratt & Whitney R-2800-8 radial engine, the Corsair raced through the hostile skies of the Pacific theater, terrorizing the Japanese with a commanding eleven to one kill/loss ratio. The plane's inverted gull wing shape made the Corsair easily recognizable. Also, its pronounced whining sound as it gained speed in an attack gave it the fearsome nickname of "Whistling Death." This pair of "bent-winged" fighters speed past an air show audience, producing the distinctive Corsair whine. (Chino, 1989)

Right: The Curtiss P-40 has been immortalized by the American Volunteer Group (AVG), popularly known as the Flying Tigers. This P-40 is a quarter of the way through a beautifully executed slow roll performed by former astronaut Joe Engle. Note the Nationalist Chinese markings on the wings. The Flying Tigers were commanded by the strict disciplinarian Claire Chennault. Although the P-40 was hobbled by inferior performance and although the AVG was vastly outnumbered, Chennault's tactics and the pilots' gutsiness produced the lopsided score of 286 Japanese planes downed against only 23 AVG planes lost. Incredibly, 39 of the Flying Tigers' pilots became aces. The image of the shark-mouth P-40 purring across the air show line rekindles memories for many veterans in attendance. (Harlingen, 1987)

Above and right: Usually preceded by casual Hawaiian music, reflecting a calm before the storm, the Harlingen announcer breaks in on the public address system, intoning that some unidentified aircraft are approaching. As the air show crowd catches on, an air raid siren begins to blare and a wave of Zero look-alikes descends upon Rebel Field. Pyrotechnics experts then ignite explosives safely distant from the audience, causing repeated loud blasts and dark clouds rising into the sky as the attackers criss-cross the airport spewing plumes of white smoke. The CAF has begun to hold its amazing annual air show at its new headquarters in Midland, Texas. Parts of the show may be viewed as melodramatic, but the action is chillingly realistic – about as close as one could come to the real thing without ever really being in danger. (Harlingen, 1989)

Left: The Confederate Air Force is a nonprofit group dedicated to preserving the history of World War II air combat by keeping as many warbirds as possible from that era flying. For years at its former headquarters in Harlingen, Texas, near the banks of the Rio Grande, the CAF reenacted many of the major air battles of the war. Its major drama was always the re-creation of the Japanese raid on Pearl Harbor which the show's officials dubbed the Tora Tora Tora act, borrowing from the feature film of the same name. Many aircraft have been restored to resemble carrier-borne Japanese fighters and bombers used on December 7, 1941. This is a North American T-6 trainer modified and painted to look like a Mitsubishi A6M2 Zeke, or better known as the Zero. (Harlingen, 1989)

OPPOSITE:

Above: Increasingly since the late 1980s, military aircraft from behind the ill-fated "Iron Curtain" have emerged in the U.S. A popular radial engined example is the Yakovlev Yak-11. With the furtherance of glasnost, it was not uncommon to see these types decorated in old national insignia. In recent years, some Yak-11s have even taken to the racing circuit. More of these sleek planes are showing up and adding a new dimension to a growing list of U.S. air shows. (Sun 'n Fun, 1990) *Below:* Larry Bell guided his company through some of the most challenging and exciting times in aviation history, offering among the most innovative and far-reaching designs. In the 1930s, Bell designed an airplane around the 37mm T-9 cannon. The gun was mounted in the nose while the Allison engine occupied the fuselage mid section aft of the pilot's seat. An extension shaft drove the propeller. Like the P-38, this fighter, the P-39 Airacobra, had tricycle landing gear. Unfortunately, this radical departure from accepted fighter configurations was plagued with some inherent limitations that made its handling qualities fairly tricky. It ultimately found its calling as an effective ground attack aircraft, especially for the Russians who used the large nose-mounted cannon successfully against the tanks of Nazi Panzer divisions. Shown here is an improved and redesigned version known as the P-63 Kingcobra. (Harlingen, 1989)

Below: Seeking as much authenticity as possible for its huge annual warbird air show, the CAF and certain of its members have gone to great lengths to provide the replica Japanese aircraft with convincing paint schemes. Up close, an old timer or a zealous aviation buff might be able to tell that the purported Nakajima B5N Kate torpedo bomber is really a modified Vultee BT-13 Vibrator, but the splashy camouflage pattern and rising sun banner waving from the opened canopy pervade the field with a persuasive World War II feeling. When the replica Kates take to the Texas sky in concert with their replica Zero escorts, organized aerial pandemonium breaks out. (Harlingen, 1989)

Attackers

While appearing to be a wild mish-mash of independent bombing runs and dogfights, the participating pilots in the annual CAF Airsho' are experienced and well briefed. Their trick is to make the air battles come across as real with all the noise and confusion typical of combat while in fact following a carefully orchestrated script that invariably lasts for as long as the pyrotechnics technicians on the ground have explosives to ignite. Although dreadfully lethal some fifty years ago, the Kate torpedo bombers as reproduced here radiate a simple elegance. (Harlingen, 1987)

When the Allied outlook was bleak in the early days of World War II, there emerged from the hangar bays of the American carriers steaming in the Pacific a new dive bomber that offered the free world another chance to reclaim its position over the forces of tyranny. Known as the SBD for Scout Bomber Douglas, the aerodynamically clean Dauntless had recently joined the fleet in an operational capacity and in significant numbers. At the Battle of Midway in June 1942, this simple but efficacious dive bomber succeeded in saving the day. Four Japanese aircraft carriers were sunk in the battle, and at last it seemed that the tide of the Pacific war was changing. This very rare flying SBD had just come off an extensive restoration, and to keep its shine is getting some extra polishing after the flight of the day. (Chino, 1989)

In a class by itself, the Douglas Dauntless was inspired by the great Jack Northrop and designed by the brilliant high school dropout at the Douglas El Segundo plant, Ed Heinemann. The SBD could deliver its bomb load with a high degree of accuracy in steep vertical dives. On the way down, the pilot would flip open the "Swiss cheese" dive brakes, perforated flap-like devices, that would prevent the airplane from overspeeding. This design innovation is visible here. (Harlingen, 1989)

This is the world's only flying example of the Curtiss SB2C Helldiver. It is pictured here cruising a respectable altitude above the air show line at the big CAF show in Harlingen as typical Gulf Coast cumulus clouds billow into the afternoon sky. The Helldiver first saw combat in November 1943. It began replacing some of the older Dauntlesses as the war continued to unfold. Just over 7,000 Helldivers were produced. The fact that only one remains flyable is a sad commentary on the rapidity with which machines that have seemingly lost their usefulness may be disposed. (Harlingen, 1989)

Almost looking as if it might be on a torpedo run, this TBM finesses its way over the air show line in such a way as to show off its massive structure. Solid as a rock, the TBF/TBM possessed all the durability for which the aircraft of the Grumman Ironworks were famous. Many an Avenger was riddled by flak or enemy fighters and returned its crew to the safety of the carrier deck. (Harlingen, 1989)

Another product from the fertile drafting tables of Ed Heinemann's design team at Douglas, the AD (for Attack Douglas and also referred to as Able Dog) became known as the Skyraider. Too late for entry in World War II, the Skyraider served in Korea and Vietnam. Like all Heinemann naval attack aircraft it incorporated the principles of simplicity, straight forward flight characteristics, ease of maintenance, and economy. For a single-engined, carrier-based plane the Skyraider carried a sizable bomb load. Its simple design with an air-cooled engine permitted it to endure extraordinary abuse from enemy firepower. In Vietnam, the Air Force used the Skyraider to fly cover for rescue helicopters evacuating downed airmen from hostile territory. In this mission, the Skyriader became known as a Sandy or Spad. (Chino, 1989)

In its long line of distinguished naval aircraft Grumman contributed the fine TBF Avenger, a consummate attack aircraft. A big airplane, weighing almost nine tons on takeoff with a crew of three, the Avenger lumbered through the sky powered by a 1,900 hp Wright R-2600-20 radial engine. General Motors, through its Eastern Division, built a version of the Avenger known as the TBM under license from Grumman. Seen here is a TBM that survived combat in the Pacific. It was restored to resemble the Avenger piloted by then Lieutenant (j.g.) George H.W. Bush from the U.S.S. SAN JACINTO. This TBM was meticulously restored by air show veteran Virgil "Coke" Stuart, who can be seen in khaki flight suit tending to details atop his mammoth warbird. Coke enjoyed the spotlight that his restoration fostered. He and his special plane were showcased on a float in President Bush's 1989 inaugaral parade. But, sadly, Coke whose regular performances in an old Stearman and then in the "Bush TBM" delighted thousands on the air show circuit passed away. Although Coke is sorely missed, his TBM is still at times seen on the air show circuit. (Tico, 1989)

Transports

The time-honored tradition of conspicuously plastering the manufacturer's logo and slogan on airplanes of old is proudly in evidence when it comes to warbirds on the air show circuit today. This bold emblem on an engine nacelle advertises the powerplant's maker, Pratt & Whitney, a company that produced some of the most powerful radial engines and which today supplies high-tech afterburning turbines for supersonic fighters. (Sun 'n Fun, 1989)

Right: Certain aircraft that evolved in the 1930s represented a major leap forward in aeronautical design, bridging the gap between aviation's tentative beginning and the maturation of the piston-powered plane in world war. These designs sometimes evoked the description "revolutionary." Their shapes were unlike any seen before and they incorporated materials unkown or even unthinkable only a generation earlier. Propulsion systems were at last available that could provide the horsepower necessary to achieve meaningful breakthroughs in range, endurance, and payload. While appearing sleek and "modern" to the observer of the day, many of these lovely 1930s creations are today viewed affectionately as having a funkiness what with their bulbous protrusions and art deco inspired features. Emanating from the newly developed design theories of the inter-war years of the Golden Age of Flight, a twin Lockheed is shown here in an unorthodox perspective. (Tico, 1992)

The same twin Lockheed as on the previous page, named SWEET CHARLOTTE, is a regular on the air show circuit. Its interior, appointed as a VIP transport replete with glove leather upholstery, is as sparkingly maintained as the more conspicuous exterior. The aircraft's tail bears the trademark multiple fin arrangement. As a newly hired Lockheed engineer, fresh from the University of Michigan, Kelly Johnson, based on his student wind tunnel tests, adamantly advocated twin vertical surfaces for the tail of an early 1930s Lockheed airliner. Despite initial opposition from the older members of the design team, Johnson's tests proved the twin tail advantageous. Consequently, Lockheed's series of multi-engined aircraft incorporated multiple finned tails through the Constellation transport/airliner. (Sun 'n Fun, 1989)

When Bobby Younkin, son of well-known aircraft restorer Jim Younkin, hit the air show circuit in recent years with a militarized Beech Model 18 doing an aerobatic routine, audiences were mesmerized since the twin-engined Beech is not normally perceived as an aerobatic plane. Barrel rolling this twin, conceived as a transport and military trainer, delights air show spectators. As the Beech flips over on its back, the dual plumes of white smoke can be seem puffing out the engines' exhaust stacks. (Sun 'n Fun, 1992)

The tri-motor Junkers Ju 52 shown here is operated by the CAF Indiana Wing. Hugo Junkers, the forward-thinking German designer, saw the possibilities of all-metal construction long before most in the aviation community and, in fact, was producing a single seat, corrugated metal fighter plane in the latter stages of World War I. Not suprisingly, the Junkers factory pursued the use of corrugated metal in later designs, notably the Ju 52, a 1930s airliner. During World War II, this sturdy and dependable aircraft served the Luftwaffe as a bomber and, more commonly, as a transport hauling a load of as many as eighteen combat equipped troops. (Harlingen, 1989)

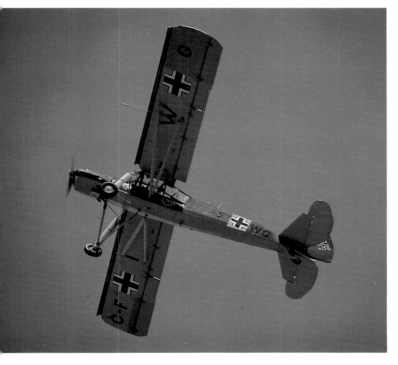

One of the most capable STOL (short takeoff and landing) aircraft ever developed, the Fieseler Storch is as close to a helicopter as conventional fixed wing planes have come. Used during World War II as a spotter plane and for shuttling officers to and from the battlefield, the Storch could squeeze into tiny pastures, making landing fields out of unlikely terrain. The few Storches flying today amaze air show audiences as their pilots will frequently chop the power and let the aircraft hang overhead almost in a hover. From this view, the enormous span and area of the wing of the nimble two-seater can be seen. (Windsor, Ontario, 1987)

A Canadian variant of the Gooney Bird (usually referred to as the Dakota in the British Commonwealth) is seen gracefully banking over the air show line during one of the spectacular annual flying events organized by the Canadian Warplane Heritage, a Hamilton, Ontario-based group dedicated to preserving World War II vintage aircraft. (Hamilton, Ontario, 1989)

In the competitive and demanding world of commercial air traffic, the Douglas DC-3 was, at the time of its introduction and for years to follow, without peer. The Douglas represented an unprecedented advance in airliner state-of-the-art, setting new standards for all passenger carrying aircraft to follow. The airplane's military application was no less auspicious. Acquired by both the Army and Navy, and known as the C-47 and R4D, respectively, the Skytrain or Gooney Bird, as the Douglas was often called, served as a troop transport, medical evacuation ship, cargo hauler, and glider tug. As recently as the Vietnam War, the U.S. Air Force used the Gooney Bird as a gunship. The award-winning restoration seen here is nicknamed YANKEE DOODLE DANDY and is operated from its base at historic Willow Run Airport in Ypsilanti, Michigan by the Yankee Air Force. (Mt. Comfort, 1987)

Right: The amphibious patrol bomber seen taxiing here is the Consolidated PBY Catalina. Ungainly in appearance, the Catalina served its World War II missions well. The bulging waist blisters provided excellent visibility and the aircraft could loiter for long stretches at a time. In the search and rescue role, the Catalina was a life saver many times over. Despite its awkward looks, downed pilots floating for hours in inhospitable waters have said that the Catalina that swooped down to rescue them was the prettiest sight imaginable. (Geneseo, 1990)

The nickname "Flying Boxcar" might sound more like an insult than an accolade when applied to an airplane. But in describing the Fairchild C-119 it is apppropriate usage. The twin boom framework sandwiches a voluminous cargo section. This design was ideal for parachute drops as the rear of the fuselage could be opened. Many of the aged cargo planes, consigned to use as civil freighters after their military service, have long since been scrapped. It is refreshing to see one, however much in need of sprucing up, appear at an air show. (Tico, 1989)

Bombers

Sometimes warbird restoration projects start with an almost incomprehensible amount of work in the offing. On the left is the Kalamazoo Air Museum's B-25 in 1989 as its restoration progress was showcased during the annual High on Kalamazoo Air Show. The air show was used as an opportunity to enlist volunteer support and raise needed funds. Three years later the fruits of the laborious effort were evident at the High on Kalamazoo event with the rollout of the colorfully decorated Mitchell, below. This top to bottom rebuild, like so many other splendid restorations of warbirds of World War II vintage, is a tribute not only to those who flew the type in combat, those who maintained it in the field, and those who conceived and manufactured it, but to the dedicated individuals who invested countless man-hours without pay or publicity to see a great airplane returned to its glorious luster. (Kalamazoo, 1989 and Kalamazoo, 1992)

This North American B-25 Mitchell is making a simulated low-level bombing run. Note that the bomb bay doors are open. It was in April 1942 that the gull-winged twin-engined bomber stamped its imprint permanently into history as the magnificent James H. "Jimmy" Doolittle led seventy-nine other volunteers from the heaving deck of the U.S.S. HORNET on the first American raid on Japan. The retaliatory strike did not inflict severe damage, but it did signal that the "sleeping giant" had, indeed, been stirred. Also, at a time when Allied morale was low due to generally depressing war news, the Tokyo raid lifted spirits at home and among freedom loving people abroad. Because the Doolittle raiders were forced to launch their attack well in advance of their scheduled departure time, none was able to make the predesignated landing fields in China. Because all crews either bailed out or crash landed, Doolittle believed that upon return to the U.S. he would be court-martialed. Doolittle's trusted crew chief tried to cheer him up, stating with fervent conviction that upon return home the government would order a promotion to general and bestow the Medal of Honor. Doolittle, who in his earlier flying career had garnered most of aviation's coveted awards, became the recipient of still more, as his crew chief had forecast. (Harlingen, 1987)

Named for the visionary military airman, Billy Mitchell, who predicted the surprise Japanese attack on Pearl Harbor, it is perhaps a fitting irony that the B-25 would be the first to retaliate on the Japanese mainland. Highly regarded by its crews and unquestionably effective in its mission as a medium bomber, approximately 11,000 Mitchells were built. (Chino, 1989)

The CAF operates today's only flying Martin B-26 Marauder. Seen here, the medium bomber banks steeply, showing off its D-Day invasion stripes. It is a mighty responsibility flying and maintaining such a rare warbird as this Marauder, nicknamed CAROLYN. Yet by flying it in air shows along with numerous other increasingly valuable warbirds, the CAF exposes throngs of spectators in an extraordinary way to an important part of history. The B-26 was initially maligned because of a rash of accidents. The aircraft did have some idiosyncrasies, but these could be overcome with proper pilot training. With time, the Marauder proved to be a worthy attack plane. (Harlingen, 1989)

The A-26 was an advanced bombing aircraft, incorporating such innovations as a laminar flow wing, but at its heart it was like all of Douglas engineer Ed Heinemann's designs – straight forward and easy to operate. It could absorb lots of punishment as it dug in low to the ground and became exposed to extensive enemy small arms fire. The aircraft was so capable that it continued to see service in the Korean War. Eventually, some surplus Invaders when sold off were outfitted with executive interiors and used as corporate planes. The A-26's speed made it a favorite of businessmen in a hurry. Other Invaders, like this one raging over Chino, California, were restored to the authentic combat motiff. (Chino, 1989)

Entering operational units late in World War II, the Douglas A-26 Invader packed an incredible wallop for an aircraft in its class. It could be outfitted with six .50 caliber machine guns in the nose as well as additional guns in other locations. Bombload amounted to 6,000 pounds. Air-to-ground rockets could be carried as well. The A-26 had a maximum speed of 355 mph, red hot for a medium bomber of the period. This Invader shares parking space with hundreds of other warbirds on a vast grassy expanse during the Experimental Aircraft Association's huge annual fly-in at Wittman Regional Airport. (Oshkosh, 1989)

This Tigercat sits majestically on the ramp prior to the flying display at the annual CAF air show. As few other airplanes, the Tigercat exudes a sense of beauty and power . . . the look of pent-up speed. (Harlingen, 1989)

The Grumman F7F Tigercat was a Marine Corps strike fighter. A proud addition to the successful line of Grumman cats, it is today a very rare warbird. This particular Tigercat is part of the Kalamazoo Aviation History Museum's flying collection. After serving as a military reconnaissance aircraft it was employed as a fire fighting plane. The restoration to the high standards of the Kalamazoo Aviation History Museum took several years. (Kalamazoo, 1992)

During World War II military strategists talked of "maximum effort", putting forth all the heavy bomber resources at the Allies' disposal and saturating selected enemy targets like the Ploesti oil refineries. With a normal bombload of 8,800 pounds, the Consolidated B-24 Liberator was one of the three leading Allied heavy bomber types that engaged in relentless aerial bombardment. The Navy was also supplied a version of the bomber designated the PB4Y. This example, dubbed DIAMOND LIL is flown by the CAF and is a peripatetic air show performer. (Harlingen, 1987)

Right: When large allied daylight bombing raids were planned for the European theater it was believed that carefully configured formations of the big new bombers, with numerous defensive positions located throughout the fuselage, would create impenetrable zones of concentrated firepower. In reality, however, swarms of enemy fighters, faster and far more maneuverable than the lumbering bombers, would wreak havoc on the formations. It was not until long range escort fighters arrived that the daylight bombers received some relief from the Luftwaffe interceptors. Seen here is the nose turret of one of the few remaining flying B-24s with double .50 caliber machine guns. The sign in the turret, reflecting warbird crew bravado, reads "Jets are for kids." The government's demand for the B-24 was so great that the production was farmed out to include Douglas, North American, and Ford in addition to Consolidated. More than 18,000 of the four-engined bombers were built during World War II. (Geneseo, 1990)

Right: This bare metal Boeing B-17 represents on a small scale the "aluminum overcast" that was created when hundreds of the durable Forts formated during World War II missions over Europe. In 1944, B-17s were no longer dressed in paint schemes but left in a natural metal finish as seen here. Operated by the CAF's Arizona Wing, this Fort is nicknamed SENTIMENTAL JOURNEY and is widely regarded as one of the most pristine among the dozen or so still flying. The hazy California sun reflects off of the plane's 103 foot, 9 inch-long wing as the stately old bomber flys on its current mission – air show passes. (Chino, 1987)

Below: Eighth Air Force B-17 Flying Fortresses, operating from fields in England, carried the air war to the European continent. American strategists were convinced that a measure of precision could be achieved in daylight missions; whereas, Royal Air Force Bomber Command, using British bombers, conducted raids under the cloak of darkness. Here a couple of air show visitors gaze at a remarkable B-17G, a later model that included a chin turret to cope with the head-on attacks of Luftwaffe interceptors. (Sun 'n Fun, 1992)

OVERLEAF:
The B-17 Cooperative consists of those organizations that fly their venerable Fortresses around the country during the air show season. Through mutual cooperation and periodic meetings, they assist one another in maintaining their aircraft. The component organizations have agreed that they will fly their B-17s to Geneseo every year in mid-August for the annual Wings of Eagles Air Show staged by the locally based National Warplane Museum, which itself operates a nicely restored Fortress. Accordingly, this annual warbird event that has over the years grown into one of the nation's largest and most prestigious warbird shows is the premier site for witnessing B-17 formations. The gentle, rolling countryside and spacious sod runway make Geneseo an optimum locale for a World War II vintage air show. (Geneseo, 1990)

The Avro Lancaster was to the British what the Liberator and Flying Fortress were to the Americans. RAF Bomber Command, led by the iron-willed Sir Arthur "Bomber" Harris, sent continuous waves of Lancasters over Europe in the last three and a half years of World War II, spearheading the night offensive. The example shown here is operated by the Canadian Warplane Heritage and is referred to as the Mynarski Lanc. When it became time for the CWH to decide on a paint scheme for its newly restored Lancaster, the choice was made to go with the colors of the Lancaster lost in combat on the night Andrew Mynarski was aboard. On that fatal mission Mynarski's Lancaster was hit by flak and disabled to the point where bailing out was the only option. With one of his crew members trapped inside a gun turret, Mynarski suffered severe burns over extensive areas of his body trying to free his fellow crew member. Sadly, Mynarski died because of his heroic efforts. He was posthumously awarded the Victoria Cross, the British Commonwealth's highest military honor. This Lancaster is one of just two flying in the world today and the only one flying in North America. (Geneseo, 1990)

OPPOSITE:

Top: World War II aircraft nose art often featured the lead pilot's sweetheart. Perhaps the most famous example is the painting on Captain Ted Morgan's bomber. His B-17 became the focus of an exalted documentary film that graphically revealed the risky task of flying the daylight bombing missions. In recent times, a feature film was based on the service of this Fortress. Known as MEMPHIS BELLE, this B-17 has come to symbolize the courage of all the American bomber crews in the war. The original MEMPHIS BELLE was extensively restored and placed on renewed static display, appropriately, in Memphis, Tennessee. The aircraft shown here is a flying replica used to play the part of the real plane in the movie.
Below: The National Warplane Museum's B-17 shown on pages 80-81 is known as FUDDY DUDDY. (Geneseo, 1990)

This amazing bomber, the Boeing B-29 Superfortress, provided a new dimension to aerial bombardment. The Superfort could carry a bombload of up to 20,000 pounds over a range of 4,100 miles and fly at a maximum speed of 358 mph. These aircraft were assigned to the Pacific theater only. The B-29 shown here is FIFI, one of the flagships of the impressive CAF collection. Obviously, the operational costs of one of these bomber behemoths are prohibitive and not surprisingly this CAF B-29 is the only one flying currently. Nearly 4,000 Superforts were built. (Harlingen, 1989)

Jets

An air show phenomenon of the last several years is the appearance on the circuit of early military jets. Restoration fever has finally spread to the warbird turbines. Jet planes dating back to the Korean War period are popping up with increasing frequency at air shows around the country. Here Rick Brickert's Lockheed T-33 RED KNIGHT swoops low and is throttled back so spectators can get a good look. The T-33 was a tandem seat trainer that evolved from the single seat Lockheed P-80 Shooting Star, the first operational jet fighter in the U.S. arsenal. Although superseded long ago by newer designs, the T-33, or T-Bird as it is sometimes called, remained in the operational inventory for many years. (Chino, 1989)

Uncharacteristically gracious looking for a combat aircraft, the North American F-86 Sabre was the leading U.S. jet fighter in the Korean War. This example, nicknamed THE HUFF, has been among the more ubiquitous vintage jet aircraft on the air show circuit. Previously part of the major jet warplane collection of the Combat Jet Flying Museum in Houston, Texas, this fine restoration along with the Museum's other seven jets were donated in spring 1992 to the Experimental Aircraft Association. (Sun 'n Fun, 1990)

The principles that for more than three decades guided the common sense design approach of Ed Heinemann were nowhere better combined and articulated than in the Douglas A-4 Skyhawk. Small, light, maneuverable, mission adaptable, simple to fly, easy to maintain, economical to produce are some of the ways to describe the attributes incorporated in the A-4. Another quality possessed of the A-4 is longevity. Conceived in the 1950s, it is to this day flying the colors of a number of air forces around the world. In the U.S., the Navy uses the A-4 for dissimilar air combat maneuver training whereby the A-4 simulates the flying characteristics of potential threat aircraft. Note the refueling boom protruding outboard from the nose. (London, Ontario, 1989)

Chapter III

Military Muscle

The screech of high performance jets causes heads to turn and necks to arch back. Modern fighters like the Eagle and the Tomcat, the Fighting Falcon and the Hornet can pass an air show audience in seconds, and even at that speed are restrained. The B-1B bomber can swing its wings. The KC-135 tanker can lower its refueling boom, simulating in-flight refueling. The Harrier can hover like a helicopter and even fly backwards. The Stealth fighter can cruise undetected, but makes itself conspicuous for air show audiences. Some of the awesome capabilities of today's combat planes are demonstrated to the public at air shows across the country. Many military installations even open their gates once a year and invite the surrounding community to come in and take a look. The uniformed men and women who maintain and fly these high-tech military aircraft usually go unnoticed most of the time, but when tensions flare in some far off corner of the world, they are the ones expected to expeditiously resolve the problem. They are the unsung defenders of our sovereign shores, the unselfish protectors of our cherished freedom. Actually, the thunderous roar of engines in afterburner is a refreshing and most welcomed sound on the air show circuit.

Fleet air defense depends to a considerable degree on the Grumman F-14 Tomcat, the Navy's air superiority fighter. Working in concert with carrier-borne Hawkeye radar patrol planes, the Tomcats provide a protective outer perimeter for the carrier battle group. Every year since 1985 Tomcats have participated in the High on Kalamazoo Air Show. In keeping with tradition, these F-14s grace the Kalamazoo parking ramp during one of the air shows. (Kalamazoo, 1990)

Popularized by the movie TOP GUN, the F-14 is, indeed, a remarkable fighter plane. Powered by two F-110-GE-400 turbofans, the Tomcat can accelerate to a speed in excess of Mach 2. Its variable geometry wing in high speed flight is swept 68 degrees, yet for the delicate maneuvering required to land at slow speeds aboard the few hundred yards of a pitching carrier deck the wings swing forward to a sweep of only 20 degrees. The aircraft's advanced radar allows the radar intercept officer sitting behind the pilot to track multiple targets and to simultaneously engage six of them. The long range AIM-54 Phoenix air-to-air missile can attack targets at distances of over 100 miles. The Tomcat has a menu of additional weaponry for closer-in aerial combat including AIM-9 Sidewinder heat-seekers and the 6,000 rounds per minute M-61 Vulcan cannon. Fast and maneuverable, the F-14 remains a challenge for any of today's potential adversaries. (Reno, 1987)

Right: A strain of thought both before and during the early days of the Vietnam War contended that close-in air-to-air combat like the dog-fighting of the two world wars was passe in the missile age where supposedly the enemy could be engaged and destroyed beyond visual range. That theory, however, evaporated in the face of air combat in the Vietnam War where American kill-loss ratios were dreadful. This circumstance spurred a return to the imparting of dogfighting skills at the Miramar Naval Air Station's Naval Fighter Weapons School, known as Top Gun. From that point, as newly trained fleet fighter pilots prosecuted the air war, the overall performance improved dramatically. This F-14, with wings swept for moving fast, belongs to VF-124, an aggressor squadron at Top Gun. (Air/Space America, San Diego 1988)

Recognizing the changes brought about by modern warfare, the U.S. Air Force in 1992 instituted a sweeping reorganization of its force structure. As was obvious in the 1991 Persian Gulf War, fighters and bombers were often flying missions with similar objectives. Despite different chains of command, these missions were exceptionally well coordi-nated. In order to foster the leanest and most responsive organization possible in the face of perceived future threats given the dismemberment of the Soviet military, the Air Force has essentially combined Tactical Air Command and Strategic Air Command into the new Air Combat Command. Some U.S. fighters, previously part of TAC, were sporting the ACC emblem at air shows as early as spring 1992. (London, Ontario, 1992)

The widely publicized air campaign of the Persian Gulf War showered attention on the long neglected Fairchild Republic A-10 Thunderbolt II. Tracing its lineage to the P-47, the Thunderbolt II shares certain of the earlier plane's characteristics. The A-10, like its namesake, is built like a tank and can absorb considerable small arms fire in the low and dirty ground attack mission. Also, the A-10 packs a devastating punch. It was designed around the GAU-8 gatling gun which can fire up to seventy 30mm rounds per second and pierce any known tank armor. In the Persian Gulf War, the A-10 actually scored more hits with infrared guided Maverick missiles launched from underwing pylons. The A-10 is not blessed with its predecessor's simple but elegant appearance, and is, therefore, referred to by its pilots as the Warthog. Several A-10s crisscross the country during the air show season providing demonstrations of the aircraft's capabilities. (Tico, 1989)

OPPOSITE:

Above: The Northrop T-38 Talon has been the U.S. Air Force's advanced trainer for about the last thirty years. Aerodynamically trim, the twin-engined fighter-like plane has a supersonic capability. The Air Force is instituting a dual-track training program in which the students pre-selected for fighters and bombers will be the only ones moving on to train in the Talon. The other students, assigned to tankers and transports, will bypass the T-38 entirely, instead flying a trainer version of the Beechjet, a corporate transport. With this new training system in place, the Air Force will reduce the usage of its T-38 fleet and extend the service life of those aircraft, putting off still longer the need for a replacement. (Selfridge Air National Guard Base, 1990)

Below: The vibrant orange and white paint scheme of this two-seat A-4 Skyhawk denotes a U.S. Navy trainer. Since the decommissioning of the U.S.S. LEXINGTON, aircraft carrier training responsibilities have shifted to the U.S.S. FORRESTAL, to which this Skyhawk is attached. For young people contemplating a career as naval aviators, seeing at an air show the aircraft one must master on the way to obtaining the vaunted "wings of gold" can be a form of inspiration. (Kalamazoo, 1992)

Designed with dogfighting in mind, the General Dynamics F-16 Fighting Falcon is a superb close-in air-to-air fighter. It incorporates the prime feature of maneuverability that fighter pilots consider essential. The F-16 is also light and has a bubble canopy which affords the pilot excellent 360 degree visibility. At the same time, the airplane, because of its adaptability, is capable of performing other missions such as close air support and air interdiction, carrying a significant bombload. The F-16 is the Air Force's multi-role fighter. Its relatively low cost and ease of maintenance ensure that it will remain for years to come a mainstay of the Air Force's operational fighter inventory. A sign of the F-16's acceptance is its service in the air forces of nineteen countries. (Air/Space America, San Diego, 1988)

A derivative of the McDonnell Douglas F-15 Eagle is the F-15E Strike Eagle, an ultra-sophisticated dual-role strike fighter. Like earlier models of the F-15, the Strike Eagle remains an air superiority fighter, but can carry a bombload of 24,000 pounds in almost any night and adverse weather conditions. Unlike traditional bombing aircraft, the F-15E has the capability of fighting its way out of harm's way should it be jumped by enemy fighters. Although not particularly stealthy with a huge mix of ordnance dangling from its underside, the F-15E was able to utilize electronic jamming means to skirt ground defenses and deliver its payload in the Persian Gulf War. This Strike Eagle is based at Seymour Johnson Air Force Base. It was one of twenty F-15s on hand at the London, Ontario, International Air Show to celebrate the aircraft's twentieth anniversary. (London, Ontario, 1992)

Rarely seen in North America is the Panavia Tornado, a large two-seat, dual-role fighter. Built by a consortium of manufacturers in Great Britain, Germany, and Italy, the Tornado is flown by the air forces of all three countries. The plane has also been exported to Oman and in quantity to Saudi Arabia. The Tornado comes in basically two versions: the ADV or air defense variant which is the air-to-air combat type and the IDS or interdictor strike form which is the ground attack type. A few North American air shows are fortunate to attract these NATO aircraft. When they show up on display, many visitors are seen scratching their heads trying to figure out the identity of the foreign planes. This aircraft, making a goodwill flyby, is an RAF Tornado. (Kalamazoo, 1992)

The Tornado is powered by two Turbo-Union afterburning turbofans that produce more than 16,000 pounds of thrust each. With its variable geometry wings the Tornado can exceed Mach 2. The IDS version can carry nearly 20,000 pounds of munitions. While displayed on the static ramp at air shows, however, the destructive capacity of the aircraft is removed from the forefront. Instead, the Tornado's novelty at North American air shows is primary. Here a crew member poses with youngsters for a picture in front of his Luftwaffe Tornado. The London, Ontario, International Air Show is noted for drawing significant NATO representation. (London, Ontario, 1992)

To virtually everyone's amazement, the Boeing B-52 Stratofortress, first flown on April 15, 1952, is very much alive and on active duty today as the U.S.'s most numerous long range, heavy bomber. Unofficially known as the BUFF for Big Ugly Fat Fellow, the B-52 is a chore to maintain and not exactly fuel efficient with eight Pratt & Whitney TF33-P-3 turbofans. This BUFF is even outliving its home, Wurtsmith Air Force Base in Oscoda, Michigan, which has been slated for closure in the recent round of Defense Department budget cuts. (Wurtsmith Air Force Base, 1990)

OVERLEAF:

This unusual perspective highlights the B-52's 185 foot-long wing span. The fuselage is itself nearly the length of half a football field. The overbearing nature of this enormous bomber gives new meaning to the expression "aluminum overcast." (Geneseo, 1990)

An attention-getter in any aerial setting, the B-52 conducted raids in the Vietnam War in such operations as Linebacker. More recently, it was flown in continuous raids against Iraqi targets in the Persian Gulf War. While the B-52 can be equipped with up to twenty air-launched cruise missiles, the bulk of the missions flown by B-52s during the Persian Gulf War involved carriage of "dumb" bombs. The massive bombloads had a devastating effect. The old workhorse has continued to prove its value after all these years in service. (Reno, 1989)

Just under one hundred of the pricey Rockwell B-1B Lancers are in service. Conceived as a long-range nuclear bomber for penetrating Soviet airspace, the B-1B is adapting to a conventional weapons mission in light of the demise of the Soviet menace. Like certain other modern military aircraft, the B-1B has a variable geometry wing which swings forward or aft depending upon the desired speed regime. As shown here, this B-1B is transitioning to high speed flight after a slow pass for the air show audience. (Sun 'n Fun, 1992)

OPPOSITE:

Above: A critical element in projecting American airpower globally is an inflight refueling capability. Without such a capability, U.S. combat aircraft would be restricted to the operational range dictated by their on-board fuel reserves. Seen here is a Boeing KC-135 Stratotanker making a show pass with the refueling boom extended. The KC-135 was developed concurrently with the Boeing 707 commercial airliner. Its large fueselage can accommodate refueling tanks with a capacity of 31,200 gallons. These planes have many times been life savers for combat crews returning from the heat of battle with depleted fuel supplies. (Wurtsmith Air Force Base, 1990)

Below: Another in the stable of aerial refuelers is the McDonnell Douglas KC-10 Extender. Based on the DC-10 tri-motored passenger plane, the KC-10 first flew in 1980. Sixty of the tankers were built, and some were modified to allow simultaneous multiple refueling from two additional points. Getting to step aboard a military aircraft is an opportunity many air show visitors gladly pursue, even if it means waiting in a long line. Here dozens of air show attendees are patiently awaiting their turn to peer into an Extender. (Wurtsmith Air Force Base, 1990)

As the "Iron Curtain" was being lifted, the Soviet Air Force, in a demonstration of goodwill, sent a small contingent of modern fighters to the U.S. The first visit of MiG-29 Fulcrums to the U.S. occurred in June 1990. Their first stop on the tour was at the High on Kalamazoo Air Show. One of the two MiG-29s journeying to American air shows that year is shown here on static display. The rarity at that time of this plane in the West caused big crowds to develop around the roped off parking area. Just about every spectator jockeyed for the best photographic angle and even Top Gun instructor pilots, their aircraft parked, ironically, kitty-corner to the MiGs, thoroughly captured the Soviet planes on video using a home VCR. The MiG-29 is regarded as a leading fighter, comparable in certain respects to the F-15. While thankfully the cold war has thawed, these high performance military aircraft are in the air forces of some potentially destablizing countries. (Kalamazoo, 1990)

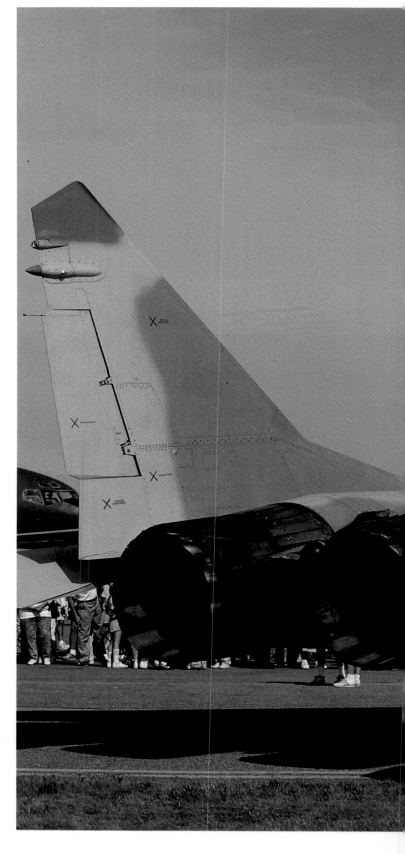

PREVIOUS:

The granddaddy of Western cargo planes, the Lockheed C-5 Galaxy occupies a bigger spot in the air show static display area than any other aircraft unless a Russian AN-124 or AN-225 should appear. The Galaxy is a gigantic strategic airlifter. Its maximum payload is 261,000 pounds, and it has a maximum takeoff weight of more than 418 tons. The aircraft's length is only about fifty-two feet short of a football field. Its unrefueled range is nearly 7,000 nautical miles. Wisely, it was designed with cargo doors both fore and aft so that ground crews could more easily load/unload the cargo. At air shows, like this one, visitors can enter the mammoth cargo plane on one end, transverse its fuselage, and exit the other end. Because of the popularity of walking through the C-5 at air shows, pedestrian traffic is sometimes directed through on a one-way basis. (Wurtsmith Air Force Base, 1990)

OVERLEAF:

Accompanying the pair of MiG-29 Fulcrums on their first trip to the U.S. was the Ilyushin Il-76 Candid, a heavy transport carrying spare parts and support crew. Its big T-tail and drooping wings can be seen here with the airframe and fin fairing of one of the Fulcrums in the foreground. (Kalamazoo, 1990)

While the Soviet Union for years succeeded in wrapping its military aircraft programs in tight security, the hard-to-get-a-peek-at fighters became almost instantly accessible to the Western eye as the vestiges of the old political system crumbled giving way to independent republics. This two-place version of the MiG-29 along with a standard single-seat Fulcrum performed brief flight routines while on a whirlwind North American tour. Decorated in the bright Ukrainian national colors, proudly representing new found independence, these planes were a pleasurable departure from the drab paint schemes typically covering fighters nowadays. This two-seater was reportedly being used to sell twenty minute rides for somewhere around $10,000 each as a means of helping to partially recoup the tour expense. Capitalism seems to be more than just creeping into segments of the former Soviet Union. (London, Ontario, 1992)

OPPOSITE:
No other aircraft in recent memory has captivated air show audiences as the Lockheed F-117A Stealth fighter. For years shrouded in mystery, the subject of speculation and rumor, the existence of the Stealth fighter was finally acknowledged by the Defense Department on November 10, 1988. Gradually, more and more revelations about the radical new plane filtered out, and following the Persian Gulf War the Stealth fighter had become a fixture on the air show circuit – the Air Force using one on each end of the country to try to satisfy the demand of air show organizers. Freakish looking, almost appearing as if it is not able to fly, the unusual shape, faceted construction, use of radar absorbing material, and special engine inlet/exhaust design provide the F-117A with unprecedented low observables that make it virtually undetectable by radar. Miraculously, during the Persian Gulf War none of the forty Stealth fighters conducting nightly attack missions over the most heavily defended targets including those in downtown Baghdad received even so much as a scratch. Meantime, their laser guided 2,000 pound bombs struck with a previously unequalled precision. (London, Ontario, 1992)

OVERLEAF:
Recognizing the probabilities of having to operate from damaged air bases or impromptu forward staging areas near the battlefield, the Marine Corps has adopted the McDonnell Douglas AV-8B Harrier II. The AV-8B is a V/STOL (vertical/short takeoff and landing) fighter. Through an ingenious design pioneered by the British, the engine thrust of the Harrier can be vectored through moving nozzles so as to allow the aircraft to fly vertically and to hover. At the same time, the Harrier is an effective fighter with an impressive arms carrying capability geared toward supporting Marine amphibious forces on the ground. In this view, an AV-8B seems to have its aim set on the Moon. (Kalamazoo, 1989)

The ultimate homebuilt, the VOYAGER, is encircled by a horde of curious and admiring visitors to the 1987 Oshkosh Fly-In of the Experimental Aircraft Association. Occupying an honored parking space just beyond the main entrance to the Convention's grounds, the VOYAGER was displayed at this annual hotbed of aviation enthusiasm as it was being trucked cross country to its permanent home, the Smithsonian Institution's National Air and Space Museum. Exhibiting extraordinary courage and airmanship, Dick Rutan and Jeanna Yeager piloted the one-of-a-kind airplane around the world nonstop, unrefueled in just over nine days. Designed by Dick's brother, Burt, the VOYAGER was conceived for the express purpose of setting this circumnavigational record. It was never flown again. This project was privately funded with the bulk of the money coming from the donations of about 7,000 supporters who came to comprise the VIP, or Very Impressive People, Club. The success of the endeavor is a tribute to the can-do spirit of individuals willing to work hard to make their dreams come true. The triumphant VOYAGER at Oshkosh on its way to the Smithsonian was one of the glorious moments in air show history. (Oshkosh, 1987)

Chapter IV

Oldies & Oddities

Air shows are self-regenerating because they host an ever-changing stable of airplanes. Invariably, a typical air show season will countenance a slew of new or unusual aircraft. Sometimes the reason is political as when the Soviet Union brought the Ruslan on a goodwill tour. On occasion, the Pentagon has relaxed its secrecy which allowed the SR-71 to appear at some shows. More often, it is the labors of a pilot or an engineer with a burning desire to make some dream of his take to the air. Mojave's king of unconventional aircraft design, Burt Rutan, has inspired a whole wave of futuristic airplanes sporting canards, tail-mounted engines with pusher propellers, and composite construction. These peculiar looking aircraft provide operating efficiencies over their traditional counterparts, and serve as the foundation for a possible new generation of air vehicles. The periodic surprises at air shows like unexpected restorations keep the enthusiasm among attendees running high. The thrill from the beauty and rarity of such airplanes perpetuates the restoration movement. When, for example, a big four-engined airliner from the past growls back to life on the ramp during an air show, one knows that a herculean effort of many devoted souls was responsible.

The ultralights area at the Sun 'n Fun Fly-In has come to be known as Paradise City. It is a beehive of activity with those who seek to stay low and slow in their flying tinkering with the "hang gliders with lawn mower engines." Ultralights and their operation are exempt from many of the regulations imposed on conventional aircraft. They offer a measure of freedom not found elsewhere in the realm of powered flight. Obviously, the economics of ultralight flight are appealing as well. The ultralight shown here sports a pre-World War II Army Air Corps trainer paint scheme, which surely plays to the warbird instincts. (Sun 'n Fun, 1989)

Maverick aeronautical engineer Burt Rutan, noted for such innovative designs as the VOYAGER, the Beech Starship, and Defense Department flying demonstrators, has had a great influence among general aviation pilots. His weird-looking airplanes offered improved performance and operating efficiencies over the more mundane shapes available on the market. These Rutan designs incorporated canards, forward wings that provide a measure of safety as they can stall while the main wings may still produce lift. The engines were located in the tail, pusher-style. Composites were used in the construction process to reduce weight. Homebuilders were anxious to build planes with new features like these that promised better performance at economical operating costs. The Rutan Aircraft Factory obliged by churning out detailed construction plans for the designs. Seen here is an example of the Rutan VariEze/Long-EZ family with the landmark Oshkosh control tower in the background. During the week of the annual Fly-In, more than 12,000 aircraft including about 2,000 show planes descend on the airport, and Oshkosh becomes the busiest airport in the world with traffic running at four times the level of peak hours at Chicago's O'Hare Airport. (Oshkosh, 1989)

A sign of the Rutan influence on general aviation is this fly-in parking area saturated with canard pushers. Many have retractable or removable nose gear. When the cockpits are not occupied, the center of gravity is such that the aircraft can easily fall back on their tails. As a result, they are usually left to rest on their noses when parked. Although the antique/classic and warbird representation has grown over the years at the big Experimental Aircraft Association fly-ins at Lakeland, Florida and Oshkosh, Wisconsin, the EAA's leaders, to their credit, have not forgotten the organization's roots, and continue to reserve the prime static display space for homebuilt show planes. (Sun 'n Fun, 1987)

Above: A special thrill of attending air shows is being treated to first-time appearances of rare or unusual airplanes. An example is the American debut of the Antonov An-124 Ruslan (or Condor), the world's largest aircraft until superseded by the An-225 Mriya. During its appearance, the An-124, which in general configuration resembles the Lockheed C-5, was flown by its Soviet pilots more like a fighter than a gargantuan transport. Of course, the huge airlifter was free of any cargo, and therefore, relatively light. Yet to see it yanked over in steep turns was an unexpected delight drawing oohs and aahs from those watching. (Air/Space America, San Diego, 1988)

Right: The Antonov An-124 is shown here making an overhead pass, exposing its underside planform. Its wing span is 240 feet and it has a total of 24 tires. The aircraft is reported to have a payload capacity of about 330,000 pounds. At its maximum weight it is said to have the ability to land in just 2,625 feet. By all accounts, the Ruslan is an impressive airplane. When the leviathan of the air first performed at the Oshkosh Fly-In, the Soviet crew waved an American flag out of one of the side windows after landing. (Oshkosh, 1989)

For a generation of general aviation pilots, the distinctive "V" tail Beech Bonanza was the "Cadillac" of the sky. No other mass produced piston-single so personified the top of the line in the light plane market as this aircraft. Many in the flying community aspired to own the Bonanza as the ultimate in personal transportation. Some of aviation's great personalities who set speed records or flew into space, cruised for fun on weekends in a Bonanza. Businessmen used the uniquely designed and easily recognized aircraft for calling on customers or inspecting plants in other cities. The "V" tail was a status symbol, pure and simple. Questions eventually arose regarding the design's structural integrity, but virtually everyone who ever owned a "V" tail Bonanza swears by it to this day. Beech still makes Bonanza models, but only with conventional straight tails. (Sun 'n Fun, 1990)

OPPOSITE:

Above: A product of the same design bureau that produces the mighty Ruslan is the An-2 light transport. Conceived long ago, but still very much in use in the independent republics of the former Soviet Union and throughout parts of the old Eastern Bloc, this radial-engined biplane is indeed slow but it enjoys a deserved reputation for reliability. Its design gives it good short field qualities. (Chino, 1989)

Below: Retired airline captain Al Chaney hearkened back to yesteryear as he operated this Ford Tri-motor on barnstorming tours around the country, selling enough rides to air show attendees to finance the trip to the next show. The "Tin Goose" in its glory days of the late 1920s elevated commercial air travel to a new level of reliability, if comfort still lagged. The Ford was slow and loud, but its corrugated metal design made it sturdy. By offering local hops in an authentic antique airliner, many people were able to enjoy a taste of commercial air travel from the early days of airliner flying. With these kinds of barnstormers, the sounds and feel of old-time flight are kept alive. (Sun 'n Fun, 1991)

When the DST (for Douglas Sleeper Transport), later designated the DC-3 (for Douglas Commercial-3), was introduced into airline service in the 1930s, passenger travel by air was revolutionized. Comfort and reliability were brought to a new standard of excellence. With the DC-3, the airlines, accustomed to reliance on air mail contracts, found that their routes could be profitable on passenger traffic alone. This old Douglas has been restored in the proud colors of TWA. (Chino, 1989)

This nostalgic scene hearkens back to an era when jet liners were in their infancy and the public was to a great extent still whisked between major hubs in big, thick-skinned, vibrating hulks that derived their power from four round engines turning windmill-like propellers. The distinctive outline of the Lockheed Constellation, affectionately called the "Connie", made it easy to spot on the ramp or in the air. The graceful lines of its fuselage arced back from the cockpit into a curva- ceous bulge like the physique of a humpback whale. The airplane's triple-finned tail made it unmistakably recognizable. Even when the airline prop jobs lost out to the more efficient jets, the Connie resisted flying off to the scrapyard. Notably, TWA continued to operate the venerable Connie on certain heavily traveled routes well after the competing lines had switched to jets. This magnificently restored Super Constellation with the wingtip fuel tanks for extended range is flown and maintained by the Kansas City-based Save A Connie Foundation. (Sun 'n Fun, 1991)

There is no shortage of attempts at innovation in the annals of aviation. One of the more inventive ideas emerged from the rubber industry at the time of the Korean War. Recognizing the need for ground troops to have a rapidly available aerial reconnaissance capability, Goodyear proposed a rubberized airplane that could be lugged in the back of a Jeep and when needed it could be inflated. Called the Inflatabird, this unconventional flying vehicle carried two in a kind of gondola up front as the overhead, aft-mounted pusher propeller provided a meager cruise. At the end of the recon mission, the contraption would be deflated and packed in the Jeep until next use. Here, on the left, Valiant Air Command volunteers are seen blowing up the craft using a portable compressor. The rubber plane is shown, on the right, fully inflated. Unfortunately, this relic does not have a current airworthiness certificate so it only serves as a static exhibit decorating the flight line. (Tico, 1992)

A familiar sight to Sun 'n Fun visitors is this permanently displayed Lockheed XFV-1 experimental VTOL (vertical takeoff and landing) aircraft. Trying to devise a high speed combat plane whose design would obviate the need for a conventional air base with runways, the Lockheed engineers came up with this ill-fated concept. Plagued with overwhelming limitations, this project did not advance beyond the flight test phase. Commanding countless incredulous stares from throngs of gawkers during the Sun 'n Fun festivities, the XFV-1 seems to at last have found its rightful place. (Sun 'n Fun, 1992)

A radically modified de Havilland C-8B Buffalo, this NASA research aircraft is known as the QSRA (Quiet Short-haul Research Aircraft). Applying upper surface blowing technology, this plane can achieve very high levels of lift and thereby takeoff and land in exceptionally short distances. At the same time, its engines, which are used in the British Aerospace 146, are very quiet. Through research like this, NASA seeks to enhance the development of commercial airliners by imbuing them with characteristics such as short field capabilities and low noise emissions that will make them successful given the realities of the current and likely future marketplace. Rarely seen on the air show circuit, the QSRA made a special visit to the Air/Space America show in San Diego from its home at the Ames Research Center. The QSRA's performance at the show did not leave anyone unimpressed. (Air/Space America, San Diego, 1988)

One of the crowning achievements of Kelly Johnson's legendary Skunk Works at Lockheed, the SR-71 Blackbird was truly an aircraft ahead of its time. By all accepted measures, the SR-71 represented the cutting edge. Its materials, structure, and propulsion systems were state-of-the-art. Though entered into service as a high speed, high altitude reconnaissance aircraft in 1964, it still holds the world's absolute speed record as of this writing. Capable of altitudes in excess of 80,000 feet and cruising speeds of over Mach 3, the SR-71 evaded enemy detection while its onboard cameras shot photos that proved invaluable to the American intelligence community. These aging yet futuristic planes were recently retired from Air Force service on the pretext that they have become too expensive to operate. There are rumors, however, that a new spy plane even more advanced has recently entered the operational inventory. Fortunately, a few SR-71s are still flying as part of an ongoing NASA research program. In the few years before the Blackbird's withdrawal from military reconnaissane missions, the once top secret plane emerged as a not infrequent performer at air shows around the country. When one of these ingenious titanium ships would come whoosing down the air show line, all heads turned with eyes fixated on the all black delta shape until it vanished high and fast. (Oshkosh, 1989)

As Reno, Nevada is the racing capital of the world, Chino, California is the leading warbird restoration and modification center. Before the burly, gas-guzzling World War II fighter remakes show their colors swerving around pylons in the high desert at Reno-Stead Airport, they are liable to be seen gradually increasing speed during progressive test hops over crop land near Chino in southern California. The air battles of World War II could probably be fought all over with the heavy iron based at Chino. When the warbirds are rolled out they include some of the finest piston racers. Seen here is the Super Corsair, a past Unlimited champion, flown by well known race pilot Steve Hinton. (Chino, 1989)

Chapter V

Resplendent Racers

During World War II, mass-produced, piston-powered airplanes were developed to their zenith. The introduction of jet propulsion revolutionized aeronautics and left propeller-driven types behind in the wake. However, the drama associated with the heyday of air racing in Cleveland, Ohio, during the 1930s has been rekindled with the annual National Air Races at Reno, Nevada. Not content to let old records stand, a stubborn cadre of pilots spends enormous time tinkering with those hot fighters of World War II vintage, striving to tweak them ever so much to squeeze out a little more speed. They have been joined in recent years by some scratch-built planes, designed expressly for competition in the races at Reno. It seems that each year these souped up piston-powered planes, in stupendous pylon races witnessed by huge crowds, are able to push the speed records slightly farther. Old North American T-6 Texans compete in their own class, and while not as fast as the modified fighters, provide exciting races as they are so evenly matched. Many of the racers are beautifully decorated in unforgettably colorful paint schemes and make walking the ramp between heats an absolute delight.

Almost all the competitors in the Unlimited Class at the Reno Air Races are highly modified World War II or immediate post-war fighter planes, such as the Mustang, Corsair, Sea Fury, and Bearcat. In recent years, a few newly designed, scratch-built aircraft have been entered into the races. One of these was TSUNAMI (translated from Japanese the name means "tidal wave"), which offered a sleek fuselage and clipped wings with a rear mounted cockpit. In many respects, the new plane, conceived expressly for the purpose of competing in the high-powered Unlimited races, seemed to borrow the configuration concepts of the early 1930's racers. TSUNAMI, in several heats at Reno, came close to capturing the Gold, but was squeaked out by the old line fighters with their pepped up engines, custom canopies, etc. Many observers believed that with time this singular purpose plane, developed and supported by racing enthusiast John Sandberg, would have won the ultimate challenge in racing, but, sadly, this promising aircraft was destroyed during a ferry flight on return to its Minnesota home. (Chino, 1989)

Reno's racers provide a potpourri of color. The huge expanse of asphalt parking space at Reno-Stead Airport is turned into a veritable montage during the four racing days in September every year. Normally, the weather cooperates, and the buckskin desert is encased in crisp air under a crystaline sky. Among the attention getters are the aged but meticulously maintained advanced trainers from World War II, the T-6s and their Navy cousins, the SNJs. These aircraft comprise a class of racer unto themselves – the T-6 Class. Race fans often find this category the most exciting because the competitors are so evenly matched. During the T-6 heats, bunches of the Pratt & Whitney powered trainers wrap around the pylons with wingtips virtually aligned as the pilots try to trade a few feet of altitude for a slight increase in speed. The race grounds are all abuzz as the North American trainers once labeled "pilot makers," throw off the noise of a factory full of motorized hacksaws from the tips of their near supersonic propeller blades. (Reno, 1989)

The waning days of World War II saw the introduction of a revolutionary new machine – the jet plane. From that point, it became merely a question of time before this new propulsion technology dominated most military aircraft. The designs that emerged from World War II essentially represented the peak in production line piston-engined aircraft. Produced at the close of the war was the Hawker Sea Fury. This aircraft and the Grumman Bearcat of similar vintage are considered the fastest production line piston-engined aircraft ever built. It is not surprising, then, to see these types with a host of engine and structural modifications engaged as racers in the Unlimited Class today. A couple of Sea Furies are seen simulating the tightness of Unlimited racing. One of the best known Unlimited racers, DREADNOUGHT, inset, is showing off in an air show pass. (Chino, 1989)

Racing planes lined up for static display make for an imposing presence. Souped up liquid-cooled and radial engines drive these large diameter, four-bladed propellers. In the foreground is past Unlimited champion DAGO RED, a P-51 Mustang painted bright red with a white/yellow accent band, and DREADNOUGHT. When these planes are powered up all at once, the ramp trembles. (Chino, 1989)

OPPOSITE:

With the exception of a few original designs, the Unlimited racing at Reno in recent years has boiled down to a contest between the sleek, liquid-cooled fighters like Bill "Tiger" Destefani's P-51 Mustang, STREGA ("witch" in Italian), above, and barrell-shaped, radial-engined fighters like Lyle Shelton's Bearcat, RARE BEAR, below. In this duel, almost every year these contenders eke out a few extra miles per hour, setting new speed records for piston-powered airplanes. As can be seen, the maintenance crews are busy in the pit area tweaking their racers for that little extra that could mean the difference between victory or defeat. These planes, including their engines, undergo incredible stresses during the pylon races at Reno. They are driven just short of the breaking point. The pilots are commonly subjected to the buffeting that comes with flying in the heated air low over the desert floor in the late afternoon. While the charging competitors jockey for position, monitoring the engine gauges and controlling stick forces soak up all of the pilots' concentration and energy. (Reno, 1989)

This close-up of a Hawker Sea Fury, DREADNOUGHT, shows its naval aviation lineage with wings folded. (Chino, 1989)

The formation flight of the Grumman cats has become a tradition at the annual High on Kalamazoo Air Show since it was first performed at the show in 1985. Representing the magnificent contribution of the Grumman Corporation to naval aviation, all the museum's cats, the F4F/FM2 Wildcat, the F6F-5 Hellcat, the F7F Tigercat, and the F8F-1 Bearcat join in formation with a currently operational U.S. Navy F-14 Tomcat. In the last few years, this unique group has been expanded to include Grumman's first jet, the F9F Panther, seen here as part of the formation. The Tomcat's wings are swept because it is on the verge of pulling up from the formation leaving a vacant slot, signifying a lost squadron member and more broadly honoring all those who have fallen in battle for the nation. The missing man formation is always an emotional tribute. (Kalamazoo, 1992)

Chapter VI

Flamboyant Formations

Another dimension is added to the demanding world of aerobatics when a performing airplane is joined by one or more in the routine. Now the pilots must not only execute their maneuvers with the same flawless precision, but must remain cognizant of the presence of their teammate(s). The civilian teams, flying everything from re-engined Stearmans to tiny Aviat/Christen Eagles, usually provide an exhibition of basic aerobatic maneuvers, both in unison and individually, including loops, cloverleaves, slow rolls, barrel rolls, point rolls, snap rolls, spins, hammerheads, Cuban-eights, and reverse Cuban eights. Some entice the audience with a series of head-on maneuvers where two team members are seemingly on a collision course as they approach each other but just in the nick of time they each execute a quarter roll providing sufficient clearance to pass unscathed. The military teams delve into their own derring-do which is all the more impressive given the size, weight, and power of the aircraft involved. In formation flying, teamwork is imperative. As the various formation teams on the air show circuit perform they exude a grace not unlike that of a well orchestrated ballet. All the elements on stage, or in the sky, are coordinated to produce an aesthetically pleasing presentation. Concentration in the cockpit is at a maximum for the slightest lapse or equivocation could be costly. Making each individually piloted airplane in the formation appear as if it is being manipulated by a single invisible controller simultaneously working puppet strings is the goal.

One of the greatest aviation museums is located in Kalamazoo, Michigan. Spawned by the efforts of prominent local citizens and veteran military flyers, Pete and Sue Parish, the Kalamazoo Aviation History Museum set out from its beginnings in 1977 to build a flying collection, not a repository of hangar queens. Today the museum exhibits about two dozen World War II aircraft, almost all of which are regularly flown. Especially noteworthy is the fact that the flying collection includes all of the early Grumman cats. It is this subgroup of former combat planes that has earned for the museum its widely recognized nickname, Kalamazoo Air Zoo. Every year at the High on Kalamazoo Air Show, the museum's contribution is apparent as its spotlessly maintained specimens are rolled out and exercised in the sky for the thousands of spectators. (Kalamazoo, 1989)

Consummate performers Jimmy Franklin and Eliot Cross have delighted air show audiences across the country with their flying antics. Mimicking World War I combat maneuvering, the two showmen in their modified Waco biplanes tear through the sky as though attacking each other. The aircraft come heartstoppingly close to each other as they cavort in their carefully orchestrated routine. Here they give the illusion of balancing one of the biplanes by resting its tail on the wing of the other. These kinds of close combined aerobatics do not leave room for even a hiccup. (Air/Space America, San Diego, 1988)

OVERLEAF:

The only four-ship Stearman formation team on the air show circuit, the Red Baron team, is sponsored by the frozen pizza company of the same name. The team's pilots, John Bowman, Sonny Lovelace, Randy Drake, and Steve Thompson, do not fly just stock Stearman trainers, but Stearmans modified with 450 hp Pratt & Whitney engines. This extra power over the standard 220 hp Continental, makes these Stearmans more agile and responsive to control inputs. They also have the raspy sound of T-6 Texans. With their smoke systems, they generate long, puffy plumes that highlight the team's precision. It is a treat to see so many big round-engined biplanes frolicking together in neat formations. The Red Baron Stearman Squadron is seen here executing flawless formation loops. (Oshkosh, 1989)

Modern day daredevils, these wingwalking teams evoke a sense of what it must have been like in the glory years of the Golden Age of Flight as barnstormers traveled from town to town performing at county fairs and staging shows from cow pastures. Jimmy Franklin and Eliot Cross hold their powerful biplanes steady as long-time Hollywood stuntman Johnny Kazian and his son arch gracefully during a formation pass. (Reno, 1989)

Flying Aviat/Christen Eagles in rainbow paint schemes, this aerobatic team is, appropriately, called the Eagles. Consisting of three great aerobatic pilots, Charlie Hillard, Gene Soucy, and Tom Poberezny, the team gives its airplanes a real workout at every air show. The little planes are highly maneuverable as proven by the superb pilots with their carefully rehearsed and wonderfully executed act. The timing and coordination of the Eagles are something to behold. The Eagles are seen here making a level pass, building speed and setting up for one of their coordinated maneuvers like the formation hammerheads. (Reno, 1989)

Using the American aerobatic standard, the Pitts biplane, the Holiday Inn team has entertained audiences at innumerable air shows over the years. Corporate sponsorshp has become a necessity for large teams as the capital and operating costs of performing in top notch equipment have skyrocketed. Indeed, it was recently announced that this team would have its traditional sponsor joined by the Coca Cola Company as cosponsor. Accordingly, the Holiday Inn paint scheme shown here was going to have the Coke logo added to it. Companies have found that having their colors and names emblazoned on the aircraft performing before large crowds across the country can be an effective method to reach prospective customers. At the time this picture was taken, the team was comprised of John Morrissey, T. J. Brown, Mike Van Waganen, and Lew Shattuck, all former fighter pilots with Vietnam combat experience. (Mt. Comfort, 1987)

Ben Cunningham, Steve Gustafson, and Alan Henley form the Jackson, Mississippi-based North American Team. Flying uniformly decorated 1940's Texan trainers, the team wakes up any dozing spectators as the three big Pratts rattle furiously during the act. These planes in formation are put through many of the same aerobatic maneuvers required of military cadets in advanced training during World War II. The team is shown here climbing vertically on the way up to a loop. (Sun 'n Fun, 1992)

Certain air show performers are known for some trademark maneuver or routine. For the French Connection team that repeated and recognized characteristic is flying extremely close during aerobatics. The closeness culminates in a mirror pass where the two French CAP 10Bs, the lower one banked and the higher one inverted, almost touch, giving the illusory image of a single biplane. These types of masterful maneuvers were concocted and are flown by Daniel Heligoin and Montaine Mallet, both transplanted from France where Daniel was the national aerobatic champion. After many years of operating from upstate New York, they are now based in Bunnell, Florida. (Kalamazoo, 1989)

The Army, like the other branches of the U.S. armed forces, makes its presence known on the air show circuit. The Army has two separate Golden Knights parachute teams. Each team has fourteen paratroopers, who although trained in widely differing specialties, must be expert jumpers. Based at the "Home of the Airborne," Fort Bragg, North Carolina, members of the Golden Knights strive to be the world's best parachutists. They regularly compete in national and international jumping competitions with rewarding results. Here one of their jump planes, a Fokker F27, makes a pass. Astounding many air show audiences with their uncanny accuracy, the Knights almost always land exactly on the spot they have pre-designated. (Kalamazoo, 1990)

OVERLEAF:
Known as "America's Ambassadors in Blue", the U.S. Air Force Thunderbirds perform up to about seventy-five shows during the air show season from March through November. The Air Force's air demonstration squadron consists not merely of the pilots of the six performing General Dynamics F-16 Fighting Falcons, but of 140 dedicated personnel who include powerplant technicians, supply officers, and public relations specialists. When not on their grueling air show schedule, team members practice the demanding maneuvers at the Thunderbirds' home, Nellis Air Force Base near Las Vegas. The Thunderbirds name derives from the mythical creature in American Indian lore that was, according to legend, a combination of man, eagle, and hawk. This hybrid, it was said, could unleash thunder from its wings. The Thunderbirds' flyers are experienced fighter pilots who exemplify all that is best in the Air Force. Their precision and skill in handling the control sensitive Mach 2+ F-16s is apparent in the famed diamond formation. (Wurtsmith Air Force Base, 1989)

Below: The Six of Diamonds team, including Jim Beasley, Daniel Calderdale, Dan Dameo, Bill Dodds, and Jerry Walbrun, has performed at many air shows using five North American Texans in varying paint schemes. Here the team's logo, as emblazoned on one of the World War II advanced trainers, is shown in closeup. (Sun 'n Fun, 1989)

OPPOSITE:

There has always been a mystique surrounding Navy and Marine pilots for in addition to being expected to fly combat missions like the pilots in other branches of the military, they face the challenge of landing on an aircraft carrier's cramped deck, the length of only three football fields, upon their return. The Navy's air demonstration team, the Blue Angels, is made up of fleet pilots who as a prerequisite must have had at least one carrier tour. The Blue Angels, like the Thunderbirds, are perceived as the best of the best by pilots in the Navy and Air Force, respectively, so there is no shortage of volunteers. The air demonstration teams provide valuable benefits that include offering the many frontline pilots who are contemplating applying for team membership an incentive to maintain sharpened flying skills, demonstrating to their fellow citizens and taxpayers the government's personnel and equipment in a dramatic and entertaining way, encouraging young people to consider a career in their country's armed forces, and serving as informal diplomats when abroad. Above, flying echelon parade in their shiny dual-role McDonnell Douglas F/A-18 Hornets, the Blue Angels show the coordination for which they are famous. Below, they have formated into the diamond. (Traverse City, 1989)

After nine years of thrilling audiences in the F-16A, the Thunderbirds opened the 1992 season in the newer and updated F-16C. While the aircraft has been improved, the pilots' same standards of excellence have not changed. The Thunderbirds are seen here flying their new F-16Cs. (Selfridge Air National Guard Base, 1992)

Flamboyant Formations

Filling the void between passes of the four-ship formations are two solo Hornets that twist and turn in almost magical fashion. These skills are honed at the Blues' home, Naval Air Station Pensacola, and at their winter home in El Centro, California. (Wurtsmith Air Force Base, 1990)

The Blues are supported by a large crew transported from show to show by a Marine Corps C-130 Hercules, affectionately known as "Fat Albert." Here the C-130 is seen in a maximum performance takeoff with the help of a JATO (jet assisted takeoff). Demonstrating the short-lived extra thrust available from the side-mounted rockets, the Herk is itself sometimes part of the act, as was the case at this air show. (Wurtsmith Air Force Base, 1990)

PREVIOUS:

From their Canadian Forces Base in Moose Jaw, Saskatchewan, the 431 Air Demonstration Squadron, known as the Snowbirds, tours the North American continent extensively from April through October each year. The Snowbirds fly the indigenous CT 114 Tutor, a proven two-seat, side-by-side primary trainer. Because the Snowbirds perform with nine Tutors, they are the largest aerobatic team in North America. Their red, white, and blue trainers, though not as fast as the fighters comprising the two U.S. military air demonstration teams, are no less graceful. In this scene, the seven core aircraft have formed a near perfect formation with equidistant spacing. (Kalamazoo, 1989)

Like their American counterparts, the Snowbirds' pilots generally remain with the team for a two-year hitch with half the team rotating each year so that transition for new members does not become a problem. Below, the full complement of nine aircraft passes in an impressive display of finesse. On the left, the entire team is seen beautifully cascading from a higher altitude, the backwards rippling trails of smoke marking an unconventional path in the sky. (Air/Space America, San Diego, 1988)

An important part of a military team member's job is interacting with the audience when the performance is over. Pilots and maintenance crew know that how they handle themselves on the show line during handshakes and autographs will greatly influence the public's perception of them and their service. Getting a smile from one of the performers after an awesome flying display can cap an intriguing day for young boys and girls as well as their parents. It is the kind of experience that stays with a person and that can inspire productive dreams and foster worthy aspirations. Here a member of the Snowbirds is providing autographs for fans young and old. (Windsor, Ontario, 1989)

Though not widely publicized and encountering its share of inclement weather, the Halcones (Falcons), the Chilean Air Force aerobatic team, enlivened five U.S. air shows during its first American tour in 1990. Interestingly, flying not a military aircraft but a version of German designer Walter Extra's aerobatic monoplane, the team's pilots fascinated onlookers with hair-raising stunts that involved skimming inverted ever so close to the ground and passing each other in opposing solos with seemingly just inches to spare in the separations. Some air show spectators were so unnerved by the gyrating Halcones that they had to turn away at the critical moments. The pilots mixed comfortably with the audience following their breathtaking performances. They did not hesitate, at the same time, to ham it up for photographers while their adrenaline was still flowing from an exotic and demanding act. (Geneseo, 1990)

OVERLEAF:
The world's largest military air demonstration team, Italy's Frecce Tricolori (meaning tricolored arrows to represent the colors of the Italian flag), made one of its rare North American tours in 1992 to celebrate the 500th anniversary of the disocovery of the New World by Columbus. Flying ten high-performance Aermacchi MB-339A/PAN trainers that are decorated in a dark blue with striping in national colors and with yellow lettering, the team cuts a large swath out of the sky. Unlike the North American military air demonstration teams, the members of the National Italian Team stay on flying with their team for extended periods – even for over five years is not uncommon. A highlight of the team's remarkable routine is when nine of their aircraft formate line abreast and emit smoke plumes of red, white, and green in symmetrical lines that fill the sky with an enormous Italian flag. (Battle Creek, 1992)

The world's largest aviation event, the annual Experimental Aircraft Association Fly-In and Convention in Oshkosh, Wisconsin, is also among the friendliest. Convention staff and volunteers putt around in a well maintained fleet of Volkswagen Beetles. Indeed, the organization's founder, Paul Poberezny, is often seen scooting about on his rounds in a bright red VW labeled "Red One." This continuing personal hands-on involvement by the group's leader in such a high profile manner helps keep the annual one week affair under control and running smoothly in the face of burgeoning growth. Despite the event's head count having mushroomed to well in excess of 800,000, there is still a pervasive homeyness, a willingness of participants and visitors to extend a helping hand. Perhaps most amazing is that when the daily air shows conclude, the grounds which were swelling with excited spectators are virtually spotless, the soft drink cups and hotdog wrappings having been courteously placed in the trash receptacles. (Oshkosh, 1989)

Chapter VII

Fanatics and Friends

Having an airplane to fly can be part of a great adventure. Having a special place to go in the airplane can fulfill the adventure. For many pilots, air shows and fly-ins serve as that special place. Those smitten by the aviation bug find flying events remarkable not merely for the incredible hardware they attract but for the camaraderie that is ever-present. There are flying buffs who have developed life-long friendships with fellow aviation enthusiasts who they met at a fly-in barbecue. Valuable maintenance tips on the care of a delicate antique airplane are exchanged at air shows between owners of the same aircraft type. Opportunities abound to participate in dawn patrols – taking off in a group for a nearby destination, enjoying a pancake breakfast, and returning to the air show or fly-in. There is a level of pride in attending shows. Some old-timers wear flight jackets festooned with the yearly patches that proclaim their uninterrupted attendance at particular events like the Oshkosh Fly-In. Some fly-ins are major undertakings with dozens or even hundreds of vendors and attendance so great that a sprawling field is required. Other events take place at rural grass airstrips. Certain air shows specialize in warbirds while still others cater to the antiques and classics. Regardless of the size or the focus, the common bond – the love of flight – is in evidence among the members of the flying fraternity. Masters of the art demonstrate their finely honed skills during the flying portion of air shows. Audiences, which may include a variety of pilots, peer upward into the limitless blue to behold the magical performances.

The heartbeat of the Oshkosh Fly-In is to be found in the expansive rows of fly-in airplanes with their camper pilots and families. For one week in early August each year the flying fraternity comes together in unmatched numbers. Acquaintances are rekindled, stories are told, flashlights are lent, friendships are made. Nowhere else is the love of flying or the bond of airmanship celebrated on such a grand scale. For the duration of the event, the spacious green fields adjoining the main runway at Oshkosh's Wittman Regional Airport become a kind of pilot heaven where the everyday cares of the world temporarily recede, giving way to a celebration of the noble pursuit of flight. (Oshkosh, 1989)

In his later years, the top scoring Marine Corps ace and Medal of Honor recipient, Gregory "Pappy" Boyington, was a frequent visitor to West Coast air shows. He would set up a table and a board on an easel that advertised his accomplishments. Stacked on the table were loads of his autobiography, which he sold in great quantities to lined up admirers, inscribing each copy. An avid smoker to the end, Pappy appeared quiet and remote, not at all the television image of the brash young fighter pilot and Black Sheep Squadron commander always proving his point in fisticuffs. Some of the old vim and vinegar could be drawn from the weathered combat veteran if air show spectators touched on a sensitive subject in conversation during a book signing. But the cantankerous hero had mellowed, often leaning back with others in attendance and enjoying the air show. Pappy, with white hat pulled over his ears and books for sale, is the center of attention in a converted hangar. (Chino, 1987)

OPPOSITE:
As with many air shows throughout the U.S., the daily shows at the Oshkosh Fly-In start with a parachuist unfurling the American flag, or in this case several flags. Optimally, the jumper deploys his flags at just the right moment so that his remaining float to the surface will coincide with the singing of the National Anthem. As he tiptoes to a landing, the final stirring crescendo should be reverberating across the field. Even before he touches down, the ground crew should be scrambling to reach up and catch Old Glory as she flutters in the air, preventing contact with the ground. (Oshkosh, 1989)

In addition to offering entertainment, air shows provide substantial potential for education. An example, is the concerted effort by many local chapters of the Tuskegee Airmen Inc. to convey the major contributions of African-Americans to the history of flight. The Tuskegee Airmen themselves made perhaps the greatest contribution by forming the first black flying unit in the U.S. military as the nation entered World War II. Segregated because of the prejudiced policies of the time, these brave pilots went on from their training at the prestigious Tuskegee Institute in Alabama to distinguish themselves in air combat in North Africa and Europe. Representatives of the General Daniel "Chappie" James, Jr. Chapter are shown here attending a warbird air show in the late General James's home state of Florida. General James was a Tuskegee Airman who despite the many obstacles encountered during a long Air Force career became the first black four-star general in the history of the U.S. military. His inspiring legacy and that of his fellow Tuskegee Airmen lives on because of the efforts of organizations like this. (Tico, 1992)

Unseen by the ticket-purchasing public are the air show's behind-the-scenes preparations, such as the pilot briefing. An integral part of any air show is a preflight gathering of the performing pilots for the purpose of reviewing information pertinent to the safe operation of aircraft during the flying display. Usually, a briefing will start off with a weather report that includes forecast conditions for show times. An outline of the performance boundaries is given, as well as traffic patterns, radio frequencies, and emergency procedures. Sequencing performers in specified time slots is also done to ensure that the show does not unnecessarily lag. Show pilots who might normally exude an aura of nonchalance while roaming through the exhibit areas, are all business during the briefing. Many take notes, and some scrawl important data like the air boss's frequency on the palms of their hands so as to be sure to have it when the time comes to use it. (Tico, 1992)

The first cropduster converted to air show use is Gene Soucy's Showcat, a modified Grumman Ag Cat. During a six month conversion, the biplane's hopper was removed and front seats were installed. Also added were an inverted fuel and oil system, engine cowling, landing gear fairings, and a wingwalking strut on the upper wing. The Showcat's eye-catching orange, yellow, and red paint scheme was devised by the wingwalker, Teresa Stokes, who happens to be an accomplished aviation artist. The husky biplane tears through the sky, weighing 1,500 pounds less than if it were loaded with agricultural chemicals in its previous career. Gene, a past national aerobatic champion, makes loops and rolls and combination maneuvers look exceedingly easy, which is one of the marks of an expert performer. Teresa, for her part, positions herself variously on the lower wing and the upper wing, always smiling and with unabashed enthusiasm. This superb pilot/wingwalker team is shown performing, below, and soaking up well-deserved applause, on the right. (Oshkosh, 1989)

Any time thousands of airplanes congregate in one place, especially if a high percentage of them are aged or exotic, probabilities are such that some repair will be necessary. In anticipation of this prospect at its large annual fly-ins, the Experimental Aircraft Association sets up temporary repair facilities. Such attention to likely contingencies has helped to make those fly-ins extraordinarily successful. Here a forlorn aircraft awaits the adroit handiwork of the fly-in's dutiful mechanics. (Sun 'n Fun, 1989)

OPPOSITE:

Above: Regarded by many in the world of competitive aerobatics as the best aerobatic airplane, the Sukhoi Su-26M is a radial-engined, low-wing taildragger. A product of the same Russian design bureau that conceived the impressive Su-27 Flanker air superiority fighter, this aerobatic aircraft boasts outstanding performance characteristics. It can climb at over 3,500 feet per minute, roll 360 degrees in less than a second, and can tolerate (if the pilot can) twelve positive and ten negative Gs. In a small way, sales of this aerobatic demon to U.S. customers are helping to mitigate the cash crunch of the Commonwealth of Independent States. At the same time, the introduction of this Sukhoi in the U.S. and its engaging flying displays, usually with the design bureau's chief test pilot, Yevgeny Frolov, in command, have served to relax on a personal level some of the longstanding tensions imposed by the cold war. As time passes, more of these excellent aerobatic airplanes may find their way to the U.S. (Sun 'n Fun, 1990)

Below: Hanging from his shoulder harness for taxi and takeoff is Craig Hosking, the world's only pilot performing inverted takeoffs and landings. Modifying a Pitts with a second set of landing gears, Craig has a choice of departing and returning either right side up or upside down. Many observers have commented on the need to constantly remember which way is which for the control inputs are just the reverse. When not providing his crowd pleasing topsy-turvy air show performances, Craig is one of the most active stunt pilots for the movies operating from his Burbank, California base. (Reno, 1989)

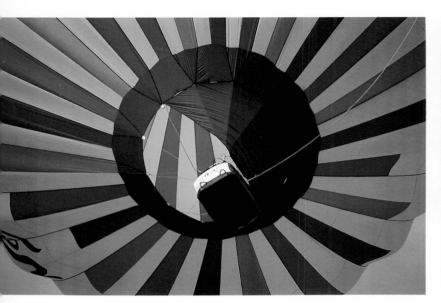

Though perhaps better known as the world's cereal capital, Battle Creek, Michigan each year hosts one of the country's larger balloon festivals. The dawn and twilight skies are punctuated with bursts of vibrant color as dozens of balloons ascend at once into gentle currents that blow them over the surrounding flat farmland. Each balloon is trailed on the ground by a dedicated crew whose responsibility is to locate the balloon upon landing and retrieve it. Except for the occasional roar of the flame-spouting burner, balloon flight is silent. Passengers in the suspended gondola are transported at nature's whim. Slowly gliding above an unblemished countryside, encircled by air, exchanging inquisitive glances with passing birds, many believe ballooning is the purest form of flight. (Battle Creek, 1989)

With a mission that includes promoting aviation as well as regulating it, the Federal Aviation Administration has taken to air show participation with, appropriately, a Douglas DC-3. A former airways inspection aircraft, the old Douglas is still jam-packed with the heavy instrumentation once used to check the calibration of navigational aids. While on static display, air show visitors are welcomed aboard to tour the flying museum. With this simple involvement at air shows, the FAA has managed to foster a measure of goodwill, give the curious an opportunity to explore the cabin of a legendary aircraft, and keep a proud old bird airworthy. (Sun 'n Fun, 1992)

The distinctive personalities among the ranks of air show performers provide an extra dimension to the air show experience. Often seen mingling with vendors and fellow performers is the ever-gracious Sue Parish, who along with her husband, Pete, provided the inspirational basis for the marvelous Kalamazoo Aviation History Museum. Recognizable in her decorative straw hat, Sue's attire belies her service as a Women's Air Service Pilot (WASP) during World War II. Imbued from an early age with a burning desire to fly, Sue overcame hurdles confronted by women seeking a life of flying. She now performs extensively on the air show circuit entertaining throngs of spectators with beautifully executed slow rolls and loops in her Curtiss P-40 Warhawk. Sporting the shark's mouth made famous by the Flying Tigers, her P-40, above, radiates a feminine touch with its pink finish. Sue, making the rounds on the right, is garbed in her flight suit that has matching pink stripes. (Selfridge Air National Guard Base, 1992 and Kalamazoo, 1989)

The Confederate Air Force is the premier World War II aircraft preservation organization. Founded in the 1950s by a small band of dedicated individuals seeking to maintain the vintage planes in flyable condition, the group has flowered and now oversees the largest collection of airworthy Allied and Axis warbirds. In order to accommodate its growing needs, the CAF recently moved from its longtime home in Harlingen, Texas to new facilities in Midland, Texas. At its headquarters, the CAF stages a spectacular annual warbird show. Noted for unabashed patriotism, CAF members proudly display the stars and stripes along with a patch of the lone star state's flag. Accompanying the national and state colors is an embroidered message reflecting the members' self-deprecating humor. It reads: "This is a CAF aviator. If found lost or unconscious, please hide him from Yankees, revive with mint julep and assist him in returning to Southern territory." (Harlingen, 1989)

Air shows have their quiet moments, too, when family and friends gather to absorb the surroundings in the peaceful shade of a gull wing Stinson. It does not get any better than this. (Sun 'n Fun, 1989)

Below: For the civil aviation fleet to remain viable, those who possess the required technical acumen must impart their talents to succeeding generations. There is no more fitting a place than an air show or fly-in for the knowledgeable technicians to pass on a taste of their trade to young, impressionable visitors. For the newly initiated there comes a sense of accomplishment in physically transforming parts needed in the repair or construction of an airplane. There is also the satisfaction in knowing that the work done on parts contributes to the successful performance of the airplane in flight. The teacher is rewarded as well, knowing that he or she has instilled an interest in young people whose involvement is vital to aviation's future. Guiding young people, sometimes literally by the hand, in the intricacies of basic aviation technology is a refreshing sight at air shows and fly-ins. (Sun 'n Fun, 1992)

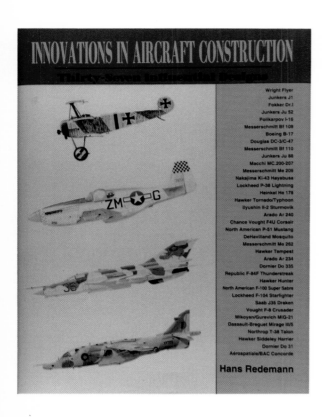

INNOVATIONS IN AIRCRAFT CONSTRUCTION

Thirty-Seven Influential Designs

Hans Redemann

Superb study of thirty-seven planes that changed the course of aviation. Detailed line drawings and over 300 photos show the development from the Wright Flyer to the Concorde.
Size: 8 1/2" x 11"   hard cover   248 pages
ISBN: 0-88740-338-7
$29.95

JAPANESE AIRCRAFT

Code Names & Designations

Robert C. Mikesh

This handbook covers all Allied designations for Japanese Naval/Army aircraft of World War II. Each aircraft is presented alphabetically according to its code name, and is also cross referenced to its official (long) designations and project (short) designations. Also covered are the non-code named aircraft and a lising of popular names.
Size: 6" x 9"   soft cover   192 pages   over 170 b/w photos
ISBN: 0-88740-447-2
$14.95

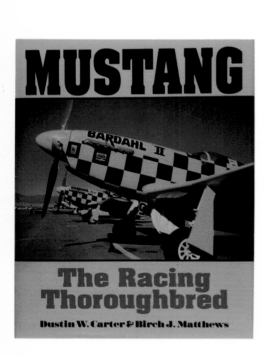

MUSTANG:
The Racing Thoroughbred

Dustin W. Carter & Birch J. Matthews

The P-51 in its post-World War II racing capacity up to the present – emphasizing engine design, speed, modifications, and personalities.
Size: 8 1/2" x 11"   hard cover   208 pages   over 180 b/w and 50 color photos
ISBN: 0-88740-391-3
$39.95

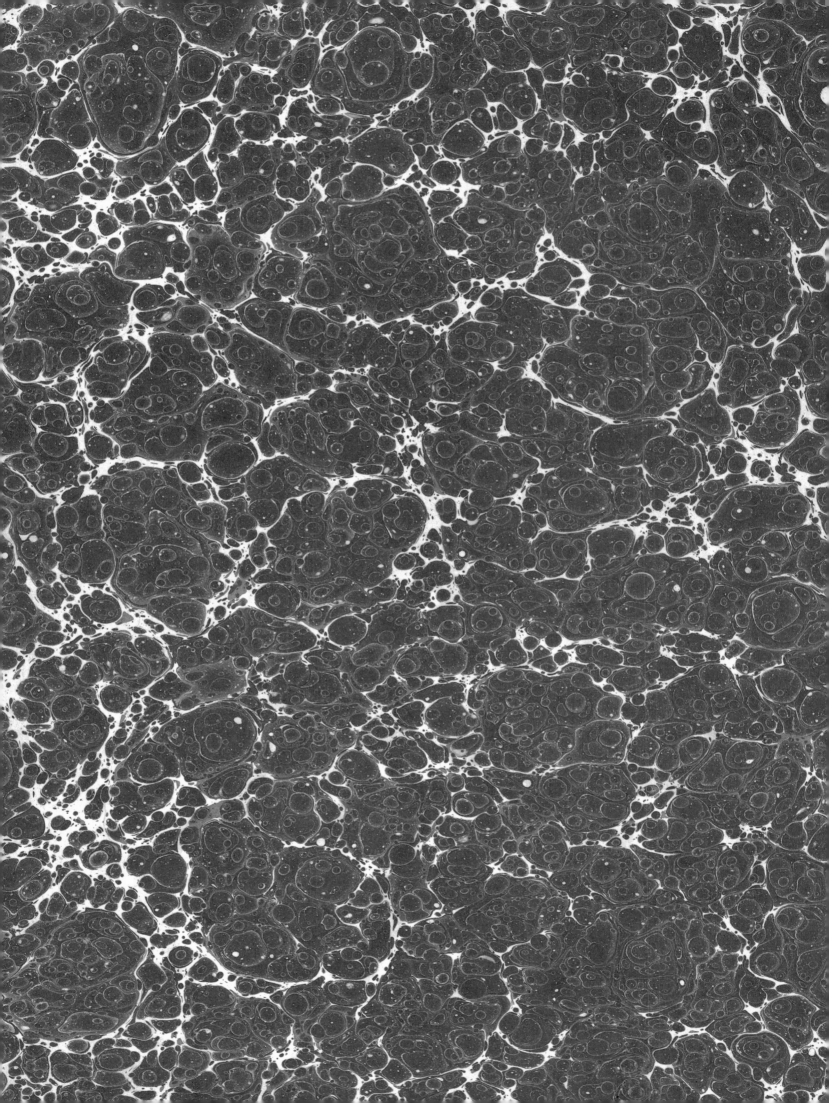